INTRODUCING
SCIENCE

INTRODUCING
SCIENCE

ALAN ISAACS

Foreword by Isaac Asimov

BASIC BOOKS, Inc., Publishers

NEW YORK

CONTENTS

FOREWORD   Isaac Asimov

INTRODUCTION

Part One   11

1   MATTER, ENERGY, AND THE UNIVERSE   13

Part Two: Matter   19

2   THE CONSTITUTION OF MATTER   21
3   THE PHYSICAL STATES OF MATTER   40
4   INORGANIC MATTER   48
5   ORGANIC MATTER   69
6   LIVING MATTER   88

Part Three: Energy   125

7   THE CONCEPTION OF ENERGY   127
8   CHEMICAL ENERGY, HEAT, AND
        MECHANICAL ENERGY   131
9   ELECTRICAL ENERGY   139
10 RADIANT ENERGY   153
11 NUCLEAR ENERGY   202

Part Four: The Boundaries of Knowledge   221

12 THE CREATION   223
13 THE NATURE OF MATTER   234
    EPILOGUE   239
    INDEX   241

FOREWORD

Isaac Asimov

ABOUT 1600, modern experimental science broke on the consciousness of Europe, and the learned world took to it with delight. Galileo's books on his discoveries were best sellers. When Otto von Guericke demonstrated the force of air pressure by fitting together metal hemispheres, evacuating them, and then setting teams of horses to pull at them in opposite directions, the Emperor Ferdinand III himself was in the audience.

In the next century, during the height of the Age of Reason, those who lectured on the new force of electricity gathered large and interested audiences. When Abbé Jean Antoine Nollet passed an electric shock through hundreds of monks holding hands in a large circle, the cream of the French aristocracy watched in interest. Louis XV himself was present at one of the demonstrations.

Nor was it only as audiences that the leisure class figured. In the 1660's, the Royal Society was founded in London, and its members were largely men of independent means who were fascinated with the thought of experimenting for themselves. They gathered together that they might describe the results of those experiments to others and listen in their turn to what those others had done. They were the 'gentlemen amateurs' of science.

What had begun about 1600 came to an end about 1800. The reasons for that end were many. First, the French Revolution had destroyed the leisurely world of the Age of Reason—that century-and-a-half oasis after the fierce Wars of Religion were over and before the fierce wars of nationalism had begun. Worse still, as wars grew fierce again, all social stability seemed gone. Aristocrats had died under the guillotine, and everywhere the threat of the guillotine's return remained. It was no time for leisure classes and dilettantism.

Second, the engineering applications of science grew more marked and important. The development of a practical steam engine by James Watt initiated what is now called the Industrial Revolution, and advances in science grew to be of primary interest to mercantile and manufacturing groups interested in production and profit rather than in abstract knowledge. To the leisured gentlemen who saw in science chiefly a new way to pursue the old aims of the ancient philosophers, that is, to penetrate the secrets of nature by experiment rather than by introspection—to these, science had become middle-class and dirty. The gentlemen amateurs retreated to the humanities.

Third, and perhaps most important, the very weight of accumulated knowledge broke down the polite support of the pillars of society. It was no longer possible to understand a scientific experiment as one might enjoy a work of art or applaud a great drama. To appreciate science, one had first to gather a background; and to do that required concentration, effort, and time.

So it came to pass that, in the nineteenth century, "professionalism" entered science. Men could no longer be scientists out of casual interest but only out of a lifetime of training and study. Indeed, it was only in the nineteenth century that the words 'science' and 'scientist' gained their modern meaning. Until then, what we call science was called 'natural philosophy'. The psychological connection with the Greek past before 1800 and the break with it after 1800 is clear in the very change in names.

The scientists themselves, conscious of lifetimes spent in training, no longer concerned themselves, for the most part, with the task of expounding their work to the general public —even to that portion of the general public which was well educated in a nonscientific sense. They addressed themselves, instead, to their fellow professionals. As time went by, the expansion of scientific knowledge was such that science divided itself into a hundred specialties, and each scientist addressed only his fellow specialists.

At no time, of course, did the art of science-writing for the general public die out altogether. Among the great scientists who (usually later in life) devoted themselves to translating the great advances of science into the common language were Michael Faraday and John Tyndall in the nineteenth century and Arthur Eddington and James Jeans in the twentieth. They succeeded famously in their popular writings and lectures.

But the audience for which they worked shrank in a relative sense as science grew either increasingly unpopular or increasingly out of touch with ordinary men. Though the wonders of physical science were all about the generations between Napoleon and Hitler, the knowledge behind those wonders was increasingly buried in higher mathematics and strange chemical symbols.

Even in biology, which, until the current generation, remained untouched by mathematics, the strange fatality of divorce from the public was maintained. The greatest advance of the nineteenth century, Darwin's theory of evolution by natural selection, roused the terror of those who feared to release their literal understanding of the words of the Bible. To these, science seemed not only incomprehensible, but evil.

In the twentieth century, a great scientific victory actually hit the front pages of the newspapers and made a physical scientist's name a household word for the first time since the days of Isaac Newton. The victory was the new theory of relativity, and the scientist was Albert Einstein. Yet, even then, one mistaken fact penetrated the mind of the general public more than anything else about relativity. This was that only twelve men in all the world could understand the new theory! All others, the popular belief went, were doomed to eternal and irretrievable ignorance.

This widening division between science and the public has often been deplored as undesirable. But, after World War II, it was no longer merely undesirable; it had become intolerable. We live in an age in which science is the overwhelming concern of everyone. This is a situation which is perhaps not good in all respects; it is possible to argue, with nostalgia, that mankind would be better off if it were not so. However, it *is* so.

And, like almost everything else for which man is responsible, science is a two-edged sword. Its every good has its evil aspects; its every evil has its good aspect. The advances in medicine that have lowered the death rate and added years to all our lives have also faced us with a population explosion that threatens to reduce us to squalor within a generation. The pesticides that have lowered the incidence of disease and multiplied our food crops also threaten to upset the ecological balance of life. On the other hand, the new understanding of nuclear forces which threaten the human race with universal destruction promises us the possibility of almost limitless energy for constructive uses.

In every direction, the choice is ours. The developments of science are, in themselves, impersonal, uncaring, withdrawn; but we ourselves can choose between life and death, between good and evil. It is not with governments only that the choice rests, nor with scientists only, but with us. Even in the modern world, even with governments we consider nonrepresentative, public opinion counts.

For many years, the two opposed nuclear supernations, the United States and the Soviet Union, have debated some sort of treaty ban on nuclear test explosions. For years, no agreement could be reached, and not because no agreement was possible. Neither side, it seemed, would come to an agreement that was not favorable to itself, and each side dreaded that an agreement that seemed favorable might turn out in the long run to be unfavorable. Neither side could achieve the maximum security it considered necessary.

Such a stalemate might have lasted indefinitely or until rendered meaningless by a nuclear war—were it not for the weight of public opinion. The vast majority of the human race fears the effects of fallout on them and their posterity. Its increasingly desperate anxiety made itself felt. If either government had wilfully refused a test ban that was not clearly impossible of acceptance on some rational basis, it would have paid the price of a vast guilt in the minds of men everywhere. Neither government was willing to pay that price, and the test ban was eventually signed.

But public opinion in matters scientific cannot exist in a

vacuum. It can be swayed by the deliberate appeals of men who wish to manipulate this powerful force to their own benefit, or it can form itself, rationally, on the basis of objective knowledge. Clearly, it is the latter alternative which is desirable.

The knowledge on which a rational and constructive public opinion may form itself can come only from the labors of those who, understanding science themselves, possess the ability to explain it to those without specialized training and are willing to spend the time to do so.

Dr. Isaacs is one of these scientist-writers. Within a small compass, without the use of mathematics, with minimum use of symbols, he manages to cover the salient areas of chemistry and physics.

Science is no mystery, and Dr. Isaacs makes it none. It is, instead, a great adventure which all of us ought to understand —if not as professional participants, then at least as intelligent and interested onlookers. Dr. Isaacs helps us do that.

If it is the great responsibility of men like Dr. Isaacs to help us, it is equally the great responsibility of the rest of us to allow ourselves to be helped.

INTRODUCTION

In our modern civilization science plays an ever-increasing part, so that to take a full and intelligent share in it each member should have at least a rudimentary knowledge of the principles involved. Unfortunately, however, the growth of scientific activity during this century has not been matched by a sufficiently widespread growth of scientific education.

Until recently the only balanced education in scientific subjects offered by our schools and universities has been the detailed courses for professional scientists. At school the non-scientific student has been treated to a very weak dose of 'General Science', or a uselessly detailed and obsolete course in classical chemistry and physics. At the universities non-scientific students have only recently been given a course in the fundamentals of contemporary science. This state of affairs recently led the Duke of Edinburgh to express the view that 'it is doubtful if the kind of science included in the general education of humanists is even barely adequate'.

This book, then, is an attempt to present a picture of the fundamental principles of science to both the adult general reader, who has not had the benefit of an adequate course in science during his formal education, and also to the school or university student whose principal interests are non-scientific.

The subject of science has been expanding in all directions at such a rate during the last fifty years that in order to produce a reasonably slender volume – not too superficial to be valueless – it has been necessary to state the present view of the facts, with only a minimal reference to the historical sequence of their discovery or discoverers. This depersonalization has its disadvantages, but it is hoped that the advantages of a purely logical approach will be of overall benefit to the reader.

From the beginning of this book no 'scientific' word is used without being first explained, although formal definitions have been avoided if they would break the logical sequence of the exposition. Furthermore, this book has been constructed on the assumption that the reader has no previous knowledge of the subject and, as the approach throughout is purely descriptive, there are no mathematical requirements.

PART ONE

CHAPTER 1

MATTER, ENERGY, AND THE UNIVERSE

WE are made aware of the universe in which we live by the action of either matter or energy on one or more of our senses. For example, our senses of taste and smell respond to direct contact with matter, whereas our senses of sight and hearing depend on radiant energy in the form of light and sound; our sense of touch can respond either directly to matter, or, alternatively, to energy in the form of radiant heat. By analysing these sense reactions, and by using our unique gift of deduction, we, *Homo sapiens*, have been able to construct a body of knowledge concerning the way in which the universe works: this knowledge is called Science.

Science, however, has never been, and probably never will be, a static collection of absolute knowledge; it has gradually developed during the recorded history of mankind, always progressing towards a deeper level of understanding and a closer approximation to the truth. For example, some 300 years ago Newton was able to explain the force of gravity in terms of the attraction which exists between any two bodies of matter; he was unable, however, to explain the causes of the forces. Fifty years ago Einstein provided a more profound explanation of gravity in his General Theory of Relativity – but a still more perfect and comprehensive theory will continue to be sought by scientists of the future. The contents of this book, then, must not be regarded as the last word in human knowledge; it does not aspire to be more than a brief descriptive survey of the state of this knowledge as it stands at the present time.

Perhaps the most fundamental advance that science has made during this century has been the elucidation of the relationship which exists between matter and energy. As we shall see later, the distinction drawn by our senses between these two concepts is much more artificial than it at first appears. The present view is that there is no absolute difference between matter and energy – that matter results when energy exists in a specialized form.

Furthermore, contrary to the old view, matter and energy are interconvertible. Thus, when an atom bomb explodes, part of the matter which it contains reverts to energy; conversely when the energy of a body is increased (for example by raising its velocity) its mass, that is the amount of matter which it contains, is also increased. However, we shall need to examine this relationship in greater detail later in this book. For the moment it will suffice to remember that matter and energy can no longer be regarded as entirely separate entities – they are interconvertible.

Nevertheless, the sensory distinction between matter and energy still remains a convenient basis for the study of the universe, and accordingly this book is divided into two sections, one dealing with matter (broadly the study of chemistry) and the other dealing with energy (broadly the study of physics). Before making a more detailed examination of matter and energy, however, it will first be necessary to say a few words about the structure of the universe with reference to the position which we occupy within it.

THE EARTH AND THE SOLAR SYSTEM

As far as we are able to tell, the phenomenon of life – at least as we know it – is limited to our own earth. The presence of life elsewhere in the universe is a possibility, but it is extremely improbable on our neighbouring planets.

The home of man in the universe then, is the earth, a sphere of matter some 8,000 miles in diameter; it is one of nine planets all of which revolve in almost circular orbits about a much more massive body – the sun. This collection of sun and nine planets is known as the 'solar system', and Figure 1 shows the names of the planets, their diameters, and the mean distances of their orbits from the sun. The diagram is not to scale and therefore gives no idea of the size of the solar system. In fact, to draw such a diagram to scale on a page of reasonable dimensions would not be possible, as the distances separating the sun and the individual planets is very large indeed compared to their diameters. For example, although the earth is 8,000 miles in diameter it is about 93 million miles from the sun, which itself is about 865,000 miles

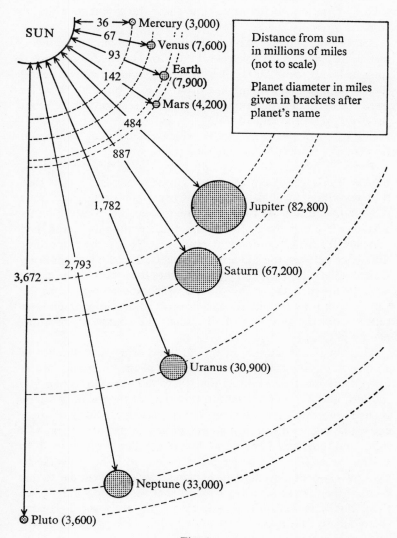

Fig. 1

in diameter. These figures give some idea of the vastness of the solar system, and at the same time show the extent to which it consists of empty space.

Some of the planets have satellite moons revolving round them, just as they in turn revolve round the sun. The earth's moon is a spherical body some 2,000 miles in diameter which revolves round the earth once every month at a distance of about 250,000 miles from the earth. These moons, however, have been omitted from the diagram for the sake of simplicity, as have also the asteroids – a ring of small pieces of matter which circulate round the sun between the planets Mars and Jupiter.

The nine planets all travel round the sun at different speeds, the earth taking 365 days to complete its orbit; this means that it is travelling through space at nearly 70,000 miles per hour relative to the sun. At the same time the earth is rotating on its axis once in every twenty-four hours, thus creating night and day.

Apart from the question of size, there is a most important difference between the sun and the planets. The sun is a hot body which radiates the heat and light necessary to sustain life on earth whereas the planets are cool bodies which absorb heat from the sun and are only made visible to us on earth by light which they reflect from the sun. (We shall discuss the source of the sun's energy in Chapter 12.)

The sun is not unique, being only one of a great number of similar stars; in order to have some idea of the immensity of the universe it must be realized that there are something like 200 million, million, million stars in that part of the universe which is visible through our most powerful telescopes. Each of these stars, like our own sun, is a source of energy radiating heat and light, and they vary in size from bodies smaller than the earth to bodies larger than the whole solar system. It is not possible to say how many of these stars have planetary systems similar to our own, as they are so far away from us that we are only able to see those bodies which radiate their own light. However, it is considered likely that at least some of these distant stars are the centre of planetary systems, and it is possible that conditions on some of these planets are suitable for sustaining life, but this is, of course, a matter for speculation.

THE GALAXIES

The stars are not uniformly distributed throughout the space of the universe, they are grouped together in gigantic clusters which are called *galaxies*. Our own galaxy is a flat disc of stars known as the Milky Way, and it probably contains about 30,000 million stars, of which our own sun is but one small and insignificant member. The nearest star to our sun, within the Milky Way, is about 25 million, million miles away (it is called *Proxima Centauri*), and the nearest galaxy to our own is about 400,000 times farther away than this.

The purpose of setting out these few facts is to see man in his true place in the universe. Far from being a central character in the cosmic plot, he occupies, as we have seen, but one tiny planet which revolves round one of millions of suns in one of millions of galaxies. It is hoped that, with this position clearly in mind, the reader will proceed to a more detailed examination of the matter of which the universe is constructed with an appropriate sense of humility.

PART TWO

MATTER

CHAPTER 2

THE CONSTITUTION OF MATTER

HAVING briefly discussed the distribution of matter throughout the universe, we are now able to proceed to a closer examination of its constitution.

Superficially, any quantity of matter, the paper of this page for example, appears to be of a continuous nature – that is, it appears to be all of one piece. An ordinary microscope, however, will disclose that paper consists of separate fibres of wood pulp closely pressed together; an even more exact examination would resolve these fibres into groups of separate particles called *atoms*. Finally, as we shall see later, the atoms themselves consist mostly of empty space, only a tiny part of which is occupied by minute 'particles' of concentrated energy. Thus, according to the so-called Atomic Theory, matter is not continuous – the smallest possible quantity of matter has a definite minimum size (the atom), and for this reason we must describe matter as being discontinuous.

By way of comparison, it should be noted that some quantities in nature are continuous, for instance *time*. Between any two instants of time, however close they are together, there is no instant of timelessness; in fact, there is no minimum size to an instant of time. We shall refer again to this comparison when we show that energy, too, is a discontinuous quantity. These considerations, however, belong to the next part of this book; during the course of this part we shall pursue an analysis of the constitution of matter and its physical states, which we shall follow with a brief examination of the main branches of chemistry under which matter is studied, namely:

INORGANIC CHEMISTRY – the study of inanimate matter.
ORGANIC CHEMISTRY – the study of matter from which living things are, or have been, made.
BIOCHEMISTRY – the study of living matter.

THE ELEMENTS

Just as all the words in our language are constructed from combinations of the twenty-six letters of the alphabet, so all the matter in the universe is made from combinations of the ninety-two 'building bricks' which are called the *elements*.

A list of these ninety-two elements is given in Table 1 together with the abbreviated symbols internationally agreed to represent them; we shall refer to the other information in this table shortly. These elements are by no means evenly distributed throughout the universe; by far the most common element in the universe is the simplest, hydrogen, but on the surface of the earth oxygen is easily the most abundant, as will be seen from the following figures, which give the approximate percentage composition of the earth's outer crust, including the seas and the atmosphere:

Oxygen	49	Calcium	3
Silicon	26	Sodium	3
Aluminium	8	Potassium	2
Iron	5	Magnesium	2

These eight elements together constitute some 98 per cent of the earth's crust; it is therefore somewhat surprising to note that the remaining eighty-four elements only constitute about 2 per cent, and such an apparently common element as copper is only present on the surface of the earth to an extent of about 0·01 per cent. The constitution of the core of the earth is not known for certain, but it is believed to consist principally of iron (possibly molten) enclosed in a mantle of dense rock, which is overlain by a thin outer crust.

The smallest particle of an element which can exist and maintain its identity is called an *atom*; there are therefore ninety-two fundamentally different types of atom. Although we shall show that atoms themselves have a definite structure and are capable of transmutation under certain circumstances, for all 'chemical' purposes the atoms of the elements are the smallest indivisible units of matter.

COMPOUNDS

While there are only ninety-two elements, there are several millions of chemically distinguishable substances, all of which are

Table 1
THE ELEMENTS

Atomic number	Element	Symbol	Atomic weight	Atomic number	Element	Symbol	Atomic weight
1	Hydrogen	H	1·008	40	Zirconium	Zr	91·22
2	Helium	He	4·003	41	Niobium	Nb	92·91
3	Lithium	Li	6·940	42	Molybdenum	Mo	95·95
4	Beryllium	Be	9·013	43	Technetium	Tc	99
5	Boron	B	10·82	44	Ruthenium	Ru	101·1
6	Carbon	C	12·01	45	Rhodium	Rh	102·9
7	Nitrogen	N	14·01	46	Palladium	Pd	106·7
8	Oxygen	O	16·00	47	Silver	Ag	107·9
9	Fluorine	F	19·00	48	Cadmium	Cd	112·4
10	Neon	Ne	20·19	49	Indium	In	114·8
11	Sodium	Na	22·99	50	Tin	Sn	118·7
12	Magnesium	Mg	24·32	51	Antimony	Sb	121·8
13	Aluminium	Al	26·98	52	Tellurium	Te	127·6
14	Silicon	Si	28·09	53	Iodine	I	126·9
15	Phosphorus	P	30·97	54	Xenon	Xe	131·3
16	Sulphur	S	32·07	55	Caesium	Cs	132·9
17	Chlorine	Cl	35·46	56	Barium	Ba	137·4
18	Argon	A	39·94	57	Lanthanum	La	138·9
19	Potassium	K	39·10	58	Cerium	Ce	140·1
20	Calcium	Ca	40·08	59	Praseodymium	Pr	140·9
21	Scandium	Sc	44·96	60	Neodymium	Nd	144·3
22	Titanium	Ti	47·90	61	Promethium	Pm	145
23	Vanadium	V	50·95	62	Samarium	Sm	150·4
24	Chromium	Cr	52·01	63	Europium	Eu	152
25	Manganese	Mn	54·94	64	Gadolinium	Gd	156·9
26	Iron	Fe	55·85	65	Terbium	Tb	158·9
27	Cobalt	Co	58·94	66	Dysprosium	Dy	162·5
28	Nickel	Ni	58·69	67	Holmium	Ho	164·9
29	Copper	Cu	63·54	68	Erbium	Er	167·2
30	Zinc	Zn	65·38	69	Thulium	Tm	168·9
31	Gallium	Ga	69·72	70	Ytterbium	Yb	173·0
32	Germanium	Ge	72·60	71	Lutetium	Lu	175
33	Arsenic	As	74·91	72	Hafnium	Hf	178·6
34	Selenium	Se	78·96	73	Tantalum	Ta	180·9
35	Bromine	Br	79·92	74	Wolfram	W	183·9
36	Krypton	Kr	83·80	75	Rhenium	Re	186·3
37	Rubidium	Rb	85·48	76	Osmium	Os	190·2
38	Strontium	Sr	87·63	77	Iridium	Ir	192·2
39	Yttrium	Y	88·92	78	Platinum	Pt	195·2

Table 1 – contd

Atomic number	Element	Symbol	Atomic weight	Atomic number	Element	Symbol	Atomic weight
79	Gold	Au	197·2	86	Radon	Rn	222
80	Mercury	Hg	200·6	87	Francium	Fr	223
81	Thallium	Tl	204·4	88	Radium	Ra	226
82	Lead	Pb	207·2	89	Actinium	Ac	227
83	Bismuth	Bi	209·0	90	Thorium	Th	232
84	Polonium	Po	210	91	Protoactinium	Pa	231
85	Astatine	At	211	92	Uranium	U	238

formed by the combination of two or more of the elements – such combinations are called *compounds*. For example, the compound water is formed by the combination of two atoms of hydrogen with one atom of oxygen. Using the symbols given in Table 1, the formula for this compound is written H_2O.

In a compound, the atoms of the elements are always present in the same proportions; thus, whatever the source of water, it will always contain two atoms of hydrogen and one atom of oxygen – no variation in this construction is possible.

The smallest quantity of a compound that can exist and maintain its identity is called a *molecule*. In the above example, one *molecule* of the *compound* water is formed from two *atoms* of the *element* hydrogen and one *atom* of the *element* oxygen. This sentence should make clear the use of the words atom, molecule, element, and compound. These words are most important in the study of matter, and the distinction between them must be clearly understood.

There is one further point to be made in this connexion. Under normal conditions, certain of the elements are gases, and these particular elements rarely exist in nature as single atoms. Usually, such elements exist as pairs of atoms combined together like compounds, and in this combined form they are also called molecules, even though the constituent atoms are of the same element.

In fact, the two elements mentioned above, hydrogen and oxygen, are both gases at normal temperatures and pressures, and they both exist as molecules each containing two atoms of their respective elements. Such molecules are called *diatomic molecules*, and they are symbolized H_2 and O_2.

MIXTURES

It is now necessary to distinguish between *mixtures* of atoms or molecules and compounds of atoms.

In nature, mixtures are very common; for example the air which we breathe is a mixture, principally of diatomic molecules of oxygen and nitrogen. Although this mixture contains very much the same percentage of each gas all over the Earth's surface (about 23 per cent oxygen and 76 per cent nitrogen by weight), the two components can be separated by such physical means as freezing (see page 46), without any chemical changes occurring to the molecules themselves.

CHEMICAL REACTIONS

For a compound to be formed, a *chemical reaction* must take place between the atoms or molecules concerned, and the resulting compound cannot thereafter be altered except by further chemical reactions with other atoms or molecules. For example, water is not a mixture of two atoms of hydrogen and one atom of oxygen, but is a compound which results from a chemical reaction between these atoms.

Using the symbols given in Table 1, it is convenient to depict the formation of a compound, or in fact any chemical reaction, by a *chemical equation*. As an example, the formation of water is written thus:

$$2H_2 + O_2 = 2H_2O$$

Such equations represent the number of atoms taking part in the reaction, and, as no atoms can disappear, the number of atoms of each element on the left-hand side of the equation must be equal to the number on the right-hand side. It is therefore necessary to make the equation 'balance', which has been done in this case by taking two molecules of hydrogen and one molecule of oxygen to form two molecules of water.

To understand the manner in which chemical reactions occur, it will now be necessary to examine the structure of the atoms themselves.

ATOMIC STRUCTURE

We have said that atoms are the smallest particles of matter which can take part in chemical reactions, and we have also mentioned that they have a definite structure. In fact, the general layout of an atom may be visualized as a miniature solar system consisting of a central *nucleus* around which revolve smaller planetary bodies called *electrons*.

The nucleus is very small indeed compared to the whole atom; so small that if the nucleus was the size of a golf ball, the atom itself would measure several hundred yards across. In fact, the atoms of the elements are extremely small, too small to be seen even by the most powerful microscopes, as they measure only about a hundred millionth of a centimetre across. As the nucleus is even immeasurably smaller than this, it will be readily appreciated that the atom consists very largely of empty space.

Electrons

Before investigating the nucleus of the atom, we must say something about electrons, which are the most elementary stable particles in the universe.

An electron is a particle of concentrated energy which has a tiny mass (1,000 million, million, million, million electrons weigh about 1 gram) and a negative electric charge. Here we are on the border-line between mass and energy, for it is probably the energy of the electric charge that gives the electron its mass. We are also at the limit of our knowledge, because we are unable to explain an electric charge – it is a fundamental unit of conception. We are, however, able to describe in great detail the behaviour of matter which is electrically charged, and it is a common experience that such charges exist in two opposite forms, which for convenience we call negative and positive. Furthermore, it is a common experience that opposite charges attract each other whereas similar charges repel each other.

We must be content, then, to accept the fact that when we

describe a particle of matter as being electrically charged, it is in such a condition that it has the property, amongst others, of attracting oppositely charged particles and repelling similarly charged particles in a well-defined manner. It must be added at this point that, although we have described the electron as a *particle* of small mass and negative charge, we must make this description with reservation. This is because, as we shall learn later, electrons are able to behave as if they were waves of energy under certain conditions. A theory has been worked out to account for this dual particle-wave nature which will be referred to again at greater length in Chapter 10.

For the present, in order to form a working picture of an electron, and in order to be able to visualize the part it plays in the structure of matter, we shall continue to regard it as a tiny negatively charged particle.

Protons

Having given a brief outline of the electron, we are now able to examine the simplest of all atoms – the hydrogen atom.

This atom consists of a nucleus with only one planetary electron, and the nucleus itself consists of one solitary atomic particle called a *proton* (see Figure 2). Like an electron, a proton

O   electron

● proton

Fig. 2

is also a particle of concentrated energy, but a proton is about 1,850 times heavier than an electron; its electrical charge, though equal in magnitude to that of the electron, is opposite in sense – that is, the proton is positively charged. Therefore the hydrogen atom itself has no resultant charge, as the positive charge of the nucleus (one proton) is exactly counterbalanced by the negative charge of the electron which circles round it. Furthermore, as the proton is so much heavier than the electron, it is obvious that nearly all the mass of the atom is concentrated in the nucleus;

this is true for all atoms, not only the hydrogen atom, as we shall see from the following paragraphs.

Neutrons

There is a further nuclear particle of great importance, which has a mass very nearly equal to that of the proton, but no electrical charge. In view of its absence of electrical charge this particle is called a *neutron*, and it is present in the nucleus of at least one form of all the atoms of the ninety-two elements. (The relation between protons and neutrons is further discussed in Chapter 11, and recent work concerning their structure is mentioned in Chapter 13.)

Isotopes

We have so far described only one form of the hydrogen atom, that in which the nucleus consists of one proton. There is, however, a second form which occurs in nature, although this second orm is very much less abundant than the first.

The second form of hydrogen is called *deuterium* (or heavy hydrogen) and in its atoms the nucleus contains a neutron in addition to a proton (Figure 3). All the elements consist of

		O electron
hydrogen	deuterium	● proton
		◉ neutron

Fig. 3

mixtures of atoms with varying numbers of neutrons in their nuclei, and these different types of atom of the same element are called *isotopes*.

It will be seen that in the two isotopes of hydrogen, the positive charge on the nucleus is equal to that of one proton, and therefore only one orbital electron is required to make the atom electrically neutral. In general, the nuclear charges of all the isotopes of an element are equal, as they always contain the same number of protons, although the mass of the nucleus will differ from one isotope to another due to the presence of different numbers of neutrons.

Atomic Number

As all atoms are electrically neutral, the nuclear charge must be counterbalanced by an equal number of planetary electrons. Thus the number of protons in the nucleus is equal to the number of planetary electrons associated with the atom; this number, which is called the *atomic number*, is a most important aspect of atomic structure, for it is upon this factor that the chemical properties of an atom depend. The hydrogen atom has one planetary electron, and therefore its atomic number is 1; the heaviest of the elements, uranium, has ninety-two planetary electrons (and ninety-two protons in its nucleus) and therefore its atomic number is 92.

The elements are arranged in Table 1 (p. 23) in order of ascending atomic number; that is to say each element contains one more planetary electron (and therefore one more proton in its nucleus) than the one before it. The significance of atomic numbers in connexion with chemical properties will become evident from what we shall say in the following paragraphs.

Atomic Weight

As we have seen, the number of neutrons in the nucleus does not alter the way in which an atom behaves chemically, because it does not alter its electrical charge, but the presence of neutrons makes the nucleus, and therefore the atom, heavier.

As the weight of an atom depends almost entirely upon the number of neutrons and protons which it contains, it is clearly of convenience to create a scale of *atomic weights* based on the mass of the proton (or the neutron). Such a scale has in fact been adopted, but it is slightly complicated by the loss of mass which protons and neutrons suffer when they combine. This small loss of mass results in the evolution of energy and is responsible for the hydrogen bomb and the energy of the sun, as we shall explain in Chapter 11. In order to overcome this difficulty the atomic-weight scale is based on oxygen, the atoms of which contain eight protons and eight neutrons giving an atomic weight of exactly 16 (for the most common isotope). On this basis an un-combined proton has a weight of 1·008 atomic-weight units, and this figure is therefore the atomic weight of hydrogen.

A second complication to this scale occurs as a result of the existence of isotopes, which can be illustrated by the element chlorine, the atomic weight of which, on the scale which we have described, is 35·457. This value arises because chlorine contains 75·4 per cent of one isotope of mass 35 (seventeen protons and eighteen neutrons – usually written Cl_{17}^{35}) and 24·6 per cent of a second isotope of mass 37 (seventeen protons and twenty neutrons – Cl_{17}^{37}). In general, in order to obtain the correct value for the atomic weight of an element it is necessary to take an average of the atomic weights of all its isotopes in proportion to the abundance with which they occur in nature. Table 1 (p. 23) gives the atomic weights of all the elements taking these complicating factors into account. It will be noticed from this table that in a few instances atomic weights do not increase with atomic numbers. This situation arises when the most abundant isotope of an element contains one more proton than the most abundant isotope of the previous element but fewer neutrons. For example, argon (atomic number 18) has three isotopes of mass 40, 36, and 38 (i.e., 18 protons with 22, 18, and 20 neutrons respectively); taking into account the relative abundance of the isotopes the atomic weight comes to 39·94. The next element, potassium (atomic number 19) has isotopes of mass 39, 41, and 40 (i.e. 19 protons with 20, 22, and 21 neutrons respectively). As the isotope of mass 39 is by far the most abundant, the atomic weight of potassium is 39·10 which is less than that of argon.

Electron Shells

In defining atomic number, it was stated that as one progresses through the elements in order of increasing atomic number, the atoms of each successive element possess one more planetary electron than its predecessor.

These planetary electrons do not cluster around the nucleus in a disorganized manner; they arrange themselves in rings, each ring being capable of containing a fixed number of electrons. These rings are called *electron shells*, and each successive shell lies at an increased distance from the nucleus. The first shell will hold only a maximum of two electrons, but the next two shells will hold up to eight electrons each. Figure 4 gives a pictorial view of the first eighteen elements showing how these electron shells are built up. This diagram is not of course to scale, and as we shall explain later such a graphical representation must be regarded as a simplification of the facts (see page 174).

In the elements with atomic numbers over 20 the situation becomes more complicated because the third, fourth, fifth, and sixth electron shells are able to contain more than eight electrons, provided that they are not the outer shell. In these elements the outer shells are able to accept electrons before the inner ones are completed, but in no case can the outer shell contain more than eight electrons. As we shall shortly see, it is the number of electrons in the outer shell of an atom that governs its chemical properties.

THE PERIODIC TABLE OF THE ELEMENTS

In Figure 4 on pages 32–3 it will be seen that the eighteen elements considered have been arranged in vertical columns so that the outer shells of the elements in any particular vertical column contain the same number of electrons (except for hydrogen and helium in which the only electron shell is limited to five electrons). In Table 3 (p. 54) all the elements are arranged in a similar manner, although after the first eighteen elements the table becomes more complicated and most of the vertical groups as they are called, have to be divided into two sub-groups designated A and B; furthermore, an extra group has to be added. We shall go into these complications in Chapter 4 in greater detail; here we need only note that they result from the effect already mentioned, whereby the third to sixth electron shells are able to contain more than eight electrons, as long as they are not outer shells.

This arrangement of the elements is called the *periodic table*, as a recurrence of chemical properties is exhibited at regular or periodic intervals, corresponding to the number of electrons in the outer shells of the elements.

The atoms of the group containing the elements helium, neon, argon, etc., all have completed outer electron shells of eight electrons (except helium which has only one shell which is completed with two electrons). These elements are called the *inert gases* because they do not form compounds of any sort, and are

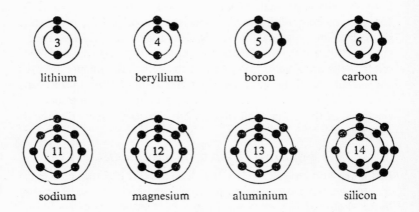

Fig. 4

unable to enter into combination with any other atoms – they are clearly, therefore, exceptionally stable.

CHEMICAL COMBINATION

The stability of the inert gases has been found to result from the arrangement of the electrons in their atoms, and we may say that, in general, atoms with outer shells containing eight electrons (or two in the case of the first shell) are extremely stable: this fact is the basis of *chemical combination*, because it is in order to increase their stability in this way that elements form compounds.

Thus, all the atoms of elements which have incomplete outer shells strive to combine with other atoms in such a way that they all finish up with outer shells containing their full complement of electrons. The inert gases already have completed outer shells, and it is for this reason that they do not form compounds.

The atoms of all the other groups in the periodic table (Table 3, p. 54) form compounds by completing their outer shells in one of two ways to be described in the following paragraphs.

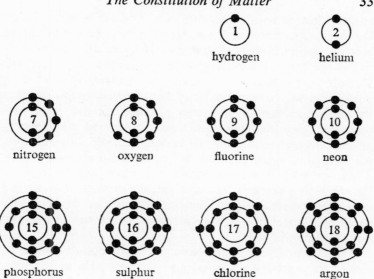

Electrovalent Method of Combination

The first way in which atoms with incomplete outer shells form compounds, is for one of the combining atoms to give to the other atom (or atoms) its odd electrons, so that both atoms end up with completed outer shells. This is called the *electrovalent method of combination* and it can be illustrated by the formation of common salt, which is a compound of the elements sodium (Na) and chlorine (Cl) called sodium chloride (NaCl).

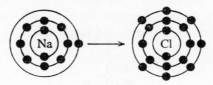

Fig. 5

Reference to Figure 5 will show that the sodium atom has one electron in its outer shell and that the chlorine atom has seven electrons in its outer shell. When these two atoms come into contact the odd electron from the sodium atom migrates to the outer shell of the chlorine atom, thereby achieving the desired result of leaving both atoms with outer shells of eight electrons. However, as a result of losing one electron the sodium atom becomes positively charged, as it does not have sufficient electrons to balance the positive charge of eleven protons in its nucleus. Similarly the chlorine atom becomes negatively charged as a result of having one more electron than is necessary to neutralize its nuclear charge of seventeen protons. As the atoms are oppositely charged, they attract each other and consequently arrange themselves into the rigid crystals of salt with which we are familiar. (Crystal structure will be explained on page 43.)

When electrovalent combination takes place, and the atoms of the combining elements become positively or negatively charged as a result, these charged atoms are called *ions*. Thus, strictly speaking, electrovalent crystals consist of collections of ions and not collections of atoms.

If such crystals are dissolved in water, the bond between the ions is very greatly weakened and they are able to separate. These ions are then able to conduct electricity through the water, by the process known as *ionic conduction*. This accounts for the familiar fact that water can be made a good conductor of eletricity by the addition of common salt, or any other electrovalent compound.

Covalent Method of Combination

The second way in which compounds are formed is called the *covalent method of combination*, and this method can be illustrated by the formation of water from atoms of hydrogen and oxygen, as in Figure 6. In this example the six outer electrons of the oxygen atom are shared with the single electrons from each of

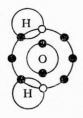

Fig. 6

the two hydrogen atoms, thus completing the set of eight electrons in the outer shell of the oxygen atom. The electrons from the hydrogen atoms in this case, however, are not released from their orbits, but are shared between the oxygen and hydrogen atoms, so that the hydrogen atoms also have complete outer shells of two electrons each.

In all covalent combinations pairs of electrons are shared in this way. For example, the diatomic molecules of both the gases oxygen and hydrogen are formed as a result of this type of combination (Figure 7).

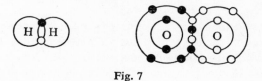

Fig. 7

Valency

All the compounds that are found in the universe are formed by one of the two methods described, or by a combination of both methods in certain cases which it is not necessary to discuss for present purposes.

Clearly, however, not all atoms are capable of entering into combination with any number of other atoms. For example, hydrogen, having only one electron, can only combine with one other atom at a time. On the other hand, elements with from two to seven electrons in their outer shells often combine with more than one atom at a time, as is instanced by the combination of one atom of oxygen with two atoms of hydrogen to form water. In order to have a working rule for predicting the number of atoms with which a given atom will combine, without going into the individual electron configurations (which, as we shall see in Chapter 4, can be more complicated than we have indicated here), it is usual to refer to the *valency* of an element; this quantity is defined as the number of atoms of hydrogen which will combine with one atom of that element.

As one atom of hydrogen can only combine with one other identical atom, the valency of hydrogen is 1; furthermore, as oxygen combines with two atoms of hydrogen the valency of oxygen must be 2. The valency of all the other elements can be found from similar considerations, and as the valency of an element depends on the number of electrons in its outer shell, each group of the periodic table (p. 54) has a characteristic valency. However, it must be added that certain elements have the ability of combining in more than one way with other elements, and consequently these elements have more than one valency. This is a matter we shall refer to again in Chapter 4.

RADIOACTIVITY

We have said that there are ninety-two fundamentally different types of atom, each of which has a different number of protons in its nucleus; in addition most of these ninety-two different atoms have isotopes, the nuclei of which contain equal numbers of protons but varying numbers of neutrons.

In our discussion so far we have regarded all these atoms as being unchangeable – existing eternally in exactly the same form, regardless of any chemical reactions in which they take part (except for the sharing and donating of outside electrons). We shall now explain that the nuclei of the heaviest elements are not stable, but are in a continual state of change to lighter elements. Such changing elements are said to be *radioactive* because during the process of decay to lighter elements they emit radiant energy. This radiant energy is of three distinct types, known as alpha (α), beta (β), and gamma (γ) radiations after the first three letters of the Greek alphabet.

An explanation of the phenomenon of radioactivity is not possible without first describing the nature of these three types of radiation, and we shall therefore say a few words about each before discussing the elements which are radioactive.

ALPHA RADIATION. This is really not a 'radiation' at all, as it consists of high-speed streams of helium nuclei. The helium nucleus, as we shall see in Chapter 11, is a very stable arrangement of two protons and two neutrons, which is shot out of the heavy radioactive nucleus intact. These α-particles, as they are called, after leaving the radioactive atom gradually slow down in the air as a result of collisions with the molecules which comprise the air, and as they do so they acquire orbital electrons, thereby becoming atoms of helium gas.

When a radioactive atom loses an α-particle, its nuclear charge, and hence its atomic number, is decreased by two units (because it has lost two protons), but its atomic weight is decreased by four units (two protons and two neutrons).

BETA RADIATION. Beta rays are electrons travelling at enormous speeds (up to about 99 per cent of the velocity of light), which are emitted from the nucleus of the disintegrating atoms. It must be made clear, however, that electrons do not exist inside the nucleus, but are created as a result of the conversion of a neutron into a proton within the nucleus. Again this is a process to which we shall refer in greater detail (Chapter 11).

GAMMA RADIATION. Gamma radiation consists of very short wave X-rays which are emitted as a result of the disturbance caused to the nucleus by the ejection of an α or β particle. The precise nature of γ-rays will be discussed more fully in the chapter on radiant energy (Chapter 10).

The Radioactive Series

All the radioactive elements which occur in nature fall into one of three separate series, each of which is headed by one of the three heaviest elements in the periodic table. The parent elements of the three series are uranium (atomic number 92), protoactinium (atomic number 91), and thorium (atomic number 90).

Each series consists of a train of transformations from one element to a lighter one, corresponding with the ejection from the nucleus of either an α or a β particle, such transformations being accompanied by the emission of γ-rays.

The uranium series, illustrated in Table 2 (p. 38), starts with the heaviest isotope of uranium, which has an atomic weight of 238. It will be seen from this table that after three α-particles and two β-particles have been lost, the element radium is formed which has an atomic weight of 226. This is because three α-particles weigh twelve atomic units (each being four units), and $238 - 12 = 226$.

Table 2

THE URANIUM SERIES

Element	Atomic number	Atomic weight	Particle emitted	Half-life
Uranium	92	238	α	4,500 million years
Uranium X_1 (Thorium)	90	234	β	24 days
Protoactinium	91	234	β	1·1 minutes
Uranium II	92	234	α	250,000 years
Ionium (Thorium)	90	230	α	80,000 years
Radium	88	226	α	1,600 years
Radon	86	222	α	3·8 days
Radium A (Polonium)	84	218	α	3 minutes
Radium B (Lead)	82	214	β	27 minutes
Radium C (Bismuth)	83	214	α and β	20 minutes
Radium C' (Polonium)	84	214	$\downarrow \alpha \downarrow$	$\frac{1}{10000}$th second
Thallium	81	210	$\downarrow \beta$	1·3 minutes
Radium D (Lead)	82	210	β	20 years
Radium E (Bismuth)	83	210	β	5 days
Polonium	84	210	α	140 days
Lead	82	206	—	Stable

The atomic number of radium is 88, which is arrived at as follows:

The three α-particles lost by the uranium have a charge of	$3 \times 2 = \quad 6$
The two β-particles lost by the uranium have a charge of	$2 \times (-1) = -2$
	Net loss $\quad 4$

The atomic number of uranium is 92, therefore the atomic number of radium is $92 - 4 = 88$. Subsequently a further five α-particles and four β-particles are emitted resulting in an atom of atomic weight 206 and atomic number 82; this atom, which is not radioactive, is the common isotope of lead. The actinium and thorium series are similar in general outline to the uranium series, and they also culminate in non-radioactive isotopes of lead.

After reading the foregoing paragraphs it may be wondered why uranium, protoactinium, and thorium continue to exist on earth if they are constantly degenerating into lead. In fact, uranium and thorium are still relatively common elements because their decay proceeds extremely slowly. The *half-life period* (the time taken for half of a given weight of an element to decay to the next lowest element in the series) of uranium and thorium is measured in thousands of millions of years. The commonest isotope of protoactinium (atomic weight 231), on the other hand, has a half-life of about 30,000 years and is consequently very rare indeed.

The half-life periods of all the atoms in the uranium series are given in Table 3, from which it will be seen that the variation is extremely wide, ranging from thousands of millions of years to about a ten thousandth of a second in the case of one of the isotopes of polonium (Radium C′).

It must be added that no chemical reaction or temperature or pressure effects will provoke a radioactive atom into disintegration, or restrain it from doing so; furthermore, the process is fundamentally an uncertain one, being unpredictable for any single atom. Nevertheless the half-life periods given in Table 3 are accurate for any appreciable quantity of matter, which will of course consist of many millions of atoms. These half-life periods are statistical averages, analogous say, to the estimated life-span of a human being as seventy years. This does not mean that any particular man or woman will die at the age of seventy, but that it is the average life of the species.

This aspect of scientific uncertainty will be referred to again in Chapters 10 and 12, and radioactive disintegration will be discussed in greater detail in Chapter 11.

CHAPTER 3

THE PHYSICAL STATES OF MATTER

I N our analysis so far, we have seen that the progressive sub-division of any quantity of matter yields the atoms of the elements, and finally the subatomic 'particles of energy' – electrons, protons, and neutrons.

We have also seen how the atoms of the elements are held together to form compounds, but we have not yet examined the manner in which the molecules of matter behave towards each other. This brings us to a discussion of the three physical states in which matter can exist, namely: the *gaseous* state, the *liquid* state, and the *solid* state. Each of the physical states will be discussed separately, as in each case the molecules and atoms of matter have a different effect upon each other.

GASES

In a gas, the individual molecules move about the space which they occupy at very great speeds, and as there are enormous numbers of them in even a small volume, they are continually colliding with each other and with the walls of the vessel which contains them. As the molecules are so small and so numerous, it is not possible to measure the speed or number of collisions per second of each of them individually. However, the behaviour of a gas can be accurately predicted by calculating the mathematical average velocity of a large number of molecules according to the so-called *Kinetic Theory of Gases*.

The pressure which a gas exerts is purely a result of the enormous number of collisions, and the high speed of impact, of the gas molecules with the walls of its container. If the temperature of a gas is increased, the molecules move more rapidly, because energy has been imparted to them, and consequently the number and violence of the collisions are increased. It is for this reason that an increase in the temperature of a gas causes an increase in pressure, and a decrease in temperature results in a decrease in pressure. In fact, the temperature of a gas is simply a measure of the energy of motion of its component molecules, as will be explained on page 131.

In a gas the movement of the molecules is entirely at random, as they are too far apart to be able to exert any appreciable force on each other. The large amount of space between the molecules accounts for the fact that when pressure is applied from outside the gas, it can be compressed to a much smaller volume.

A further fact of great importance concerning gases is that, irrespective of the chemical composition of the gas, equal volumes at the same temperature and pressure always contain the same number of molecules; this statement is known as *Avogadro's Hypothesis*, after the discoverer. Naturally the number of molecules in a given volume of gas will depend on the temperature and pressure to which it is subjected, but, if the pressure is the same as that of the atmosphere at sea-level, and the temperature is 15°C (59°F), the number of molecules in one cubic centimetre (about the size of a small lump of sugar) of any gas is approximately 27 million, million, million, and each molecule can expect to experience about 5,000 million collisions per second.

We have already stated that the earth's atmosphere consists predominantly of a mixture of diatomic molecules of the gases oxygen and nitrogen (roughly 76 per cent nitrogen and 23 per cent oxygen); from what has been said about the Kinetic Theory of Gases, it will be understood that, as the molecules are continually colliding with all the matter on the surface of the earth, they will exert a pressure uniformly over its surface. At sea-level, this pressure is equivalent to a weight of about fifteen pounds acting on every square inch of matter exposed to the atmosphere.

LIQUIDS

If the temperature of a gas is decreased sufficiently a stage will be reached when the speed of movement of the molecules is so reduced that they become close enough to exert attractive forces on each other. These forces differ from the forces that hold the

ether in a molecule, but they are also electrical in
in fact they result from the attraction between the
charged nucleus of one atom and the negatively
bital electrons of the atoms in neighbouring molecules.
Such forces are called *molecular forces* (or *van der Waals' forces*,
after the discoverer).

At that point in the process of reducing the temperature of a
gas when the attractive forces between the molecules is sufficient
to make them cohere, the gas is said to have become a *liquid*. In
contrast to solids, however, the molecules of a liquid are still
able to slide over one another, so that the bulk is able to adopt
the shape of its container.

Although the molecules in a liquid have lost their freedom to
move at random within the container they do continue to vibrate
and collide at great speeds. Nevertheless, in a liquid there is very
much less space between the molecules than in a gas and consequently liquids occupy much less space than gases; for this
reason, also, they can be compressed only slightly.

Although it is of course not possible to observe the continual
movement of the molecules in a gas or liquid with the naked eye,
the random movement of a very fine particle of dust in a drop of
liquid can be directly observed under the microscope. This movement was first noticed by a botanist, R. Brown, and is consequently known as the *Brownian Movement*. The movement of such
a minute speck of dust is entirely at random because the
collisions it suffers from the fast-moving molecules are also
random.

Some of the more rapid molecules at the surface of a liquid are
able to overcome the molecular forces of their neighbouring
molecules and escape from the body of the liquid into the gas
above it: this process is called *evaporation*. As it is the fastest-
moving molecules that escape, that is the molecules with the
greatest energy, the average energy of the remaining molecules
will be reduced, and hence the effect of evaporation is to cause a
reduction in the temperature of the liquid.

As a result of the continual escape of molecules from the
surface of a liquid, the gas above it will contain a certain number
of molecules of the liquid. This number will depend on the

temperature and the chemical composition of the liquid. However, for a particular liquid, at a particular temperature, the average number of molecules escaping from the surface will always be the same, and the pressure these molecules exert is called the *vapour pressure* of the liquid.

Clearly, the vapour pressure of a liquid will increase with rising temperature; but at a certain temperature the vapour pressure of the liquid will become equal to the pressure exerted by the atmosphere above it. At this temperature, called the *boiling-point*, the liquid is said to boil and become a gas. This accounts for the bubbles of gas that form in the body of a liquid when it boils. The above explanation also accounts for the fact that the boiling-point of a liquid is lower at high altitudes where the atmospheric pressure is lower. For example, water boils at sea-level at 100°C (212°F), but at an altitude of 1,500 ft it will boil at 98·3°C (208·9°F).

SOLIDS

If the temperature of a liquid is decreased sufficiently, the molecules are drawn so close together by the molecular forces, that at a certain point, called the *freezing-point*, the molecules themselves break down and the atoms arrange themselves into rigid patterns (called crystals), which are held together either by the electrovalent or the covalent forces which have already been described. At this point, the liquid is said to have become a *solid*.

Nearly all solids exist as crystals (see below), which when heated become liquids at a definite temperature called the melting-point of the solid or the freezing-point of the liquid. There are, however, certain solids, such as glass and some resins, which are not crystalline in nature; such substances are described as *amorphous*. Amorphous solids do not have a definite melting-point, but when heated become gradually more and more pliable until eventually they assume the fluid properties usually associated with liquids: for this reason they are best thought of as 'super-cooled' liquids.

Crystals

We have said that all solids, except those which are amorphous, exist as crystals, and we shall now discuss the three broad groups into which crystalline substances are usually classified. They are:

1. Electrovalent Crystals
2. Covalent Crystals
3. Metallic Crystals

ELECTROVALENT CRYSTALS. Such solids do not really exist as molecules, but as collections of ions held in a rigid structure by the electrovalent forces which we have described on page 33. A typical electrovalent crystal is common salt (sodium chloride – NaCl) which forms a simple crystal structure, as in Figure 8.

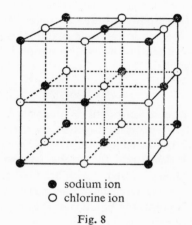

● sodium ion
○ chlorine ion

Fig. 8

It will be seen from this diagram that the ions of sodium and chlorine alternate throughout the structure, which is called a *lattice*, so that each cube formed is a repetition of all the others. Although it is necessary to illustrate the ions as occupying fixed positions, they are in fact vibrating about these positions while keeping within the general confines of the lattice.

Apart from this simple cubic structure, there are some fourteen different systems which occur in nature. Of the cubic lattices there are three different types, namely the simple cubic lattice which we have illustrated for sodium chloride, the 'body-centred' which has an additional ion at its centre, and the 'face-centred' crystal which has an additional ion at the centre of each of its faces.

We need not go into the details of crystal structure here, although it should be realized that the example of sodium chloride which we have illustrated is particularly simple as only two different ions are involved. Other electrovalent crystals, for example those of copper sulphate ($CuSO_4$), are much more complicated as in addition to an atom of copper, an atom of sulphur, and four atoms of oxygen they also include five molecules of water (called the water of crystallization). All crystals, however, are similar in principle to common salt in that the same lattice is repeated over and over again.

All electrovalent crystals dissolve in water to form conducting solutions as a result of the liberation of ions from the rigid structure of the lattice.

COVALENT CRYSTALS. Two types of covalent crystal are distinguishable, i.e., those in which the unit of structure is the molecule, and those in which the crystal itself is a giant molecule.

The first type is the more common as most organic compounds form such crystals. In these structures the atoms of the molecule are covalently linked, but the only forces between the molecules are molecular forces and consequently these crystals are softer and more readily fusible than the crystals of salts which are held together by the powerful electrovalent bonds.

In the giant molecule type of crystal each atom is covalently linked to its neighbour, and therefore such crystals are very hard and difficult to fuse. Typical of this class of crystal is diamond, which consists of carbon atoms bonded together in this way.

METALLIC CRYSTALS. In pure metallic crystals the atoms of the metal are ionized, but as all the ions are the same they must all be positively charged. Metal atoms, therefore, are not held together by either electrovalent or covalent forces, but by a special bonding of their own.

In metallic crystals the positively charged ions vibrate about fixed positions in the lattice, but the electrons which have left the outer orbits of the atoms are free to move about the crystal structure, so that the metal ions are, so to speak, immersed in a 'gas' of electrons. This accounts for the fact that metals are good conductors of electricity – the free electrons are able to carry the current through the crystals.

The theory of metal structure is a very complex subject, which has come into prominence during recent years as a result of the endurance that is required of the metal components of jet engines and rockets at very high temperatures. This subject is, however, beyond the scope of this book.

TEMPERATURE

We have said that the physical state of matter depends upon the extent of the movement and vibrations of the individual atoms or molecules of which it consists. We have also said that the energy of these movements and vibrations depends on, and is in fact a measure of, the temperature of the matter concerned.

Thus by reducing the temperature of matter in the gaseous state it can be made to pass through all three physical states. For example, steam consists of water in the gaseous state – a reduction of its temperature to its boiling-point and liquid water results – a further reduction of temperature to the freezing-point and solid ice appears (see Figure 9). While it is true that all gases can be

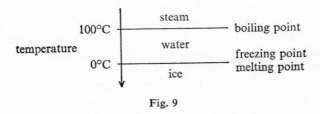

Fig. 9

made to liquefy and finally solidify, some gases will only do so at very low temperatures; for example, oxygen liquefies at −183°C and nitrogen liquefies at −195·8°C. The fact that there is a difference in these temperatures enables the two gases to be separated from the atmosphere simply by reducing the temperature of air in a special type of refrigerator. At −183°C the oxygen liquefies out, leaving mostly nitrogen in the gaseous state.

The inert gases liquefy at even lower temperatures; for example neon does not become a liquid until a temperature of $-245.9°C$ has been reached and it does not solidify until $-248.7°C$.

Although all gases will liquefy and finally solidify, not all solids can be liquefied and not all liquids can be gasified. This is because raising the temperature of some solid and liquid compounds causes them to decompose into their elements (or oxidize if they are heated in air) before they have had time to change their state.

We have said that the reduction in temperature of matter in any state reduces the movements and vibrations of its component atoms or molecules. It is only logical to assume, then, that at some stage in the process of lowering the temperature, these movements and vibrations will cease altogether. Such a temperature does, in fact, exist, and is called the *absolute zero of temperature*, although it is unattainable both in theory and practice because matter would cease to exist if the movement of its atoms and molecules came to a standstill.

The absolute zero of temperature is $-273°C$: although unattainable, it has been possible to approach to within very much less than a degree of it in the laboratory. We shall have more to say about the subject of temperature in general, and absolute zero in particular, in Chapter 8.

CHAPTER 4

INORGANIC MATTER

IN Chapter 2 we outlined the general constitution of matter in terms of modern atomic theory, and in Chapter 3 we discussed the physical states in which it exists. During the course of these chapters we have had occasion to mention by name a few of the commonest elements and their compounds, but as there are ninety-two different elements and several millions of compounds occurring in nature, it is clear that we have hardly scratched the surface of chemistry, which comprises a systematic study of the properties of all the elements and compounds.

Purely as a matter of convenience, the large group of compounds which are formed from the element carbon, and which are associated with living matter, are treated separately as the subject of organic chemistry (see next chapter), while all the other elements and their compounds form the study of inorganic chemistry with which we shall deal in this chapter. This may appear a somewhat alarming prospect, but as well over half of the ninety-two elements are extremely scarce, and therefore do not greatly concern us, the field is considerably reduced.

In Chapter 2 we drew attention to the fact that the properties of the elements can be broadly classified by arranging them in the groups of the periodic table, and it is therefore a more detailed study of this table which will mostly occupy this chapter. However, before discussing the periodic table in greater detail it will be convenient to have in mind some of the commonest types of compounds which are formed in nature.

RADICALS

In addition to compounds which are made from various arrangements of only two elements, such as we have mentioned so far, we must now refer to the very many compounds which are made from more than two elements; these compounds usually include groups of atoms called *radicals*. Radicals are formed by the covalent combination of certain elements with oxygen, and they are unstable unless they can combine electrovalently with other elements. The most common radicals are set out below together with their formulae and valency:

Radical	Formula	Valency
Sulphate	SO_4	2
Sulphite	SO_3	2
Nitrate	NO_3	1
Nitrite	NO_2	1
Carbonate	CO_3	2
Phosphate	PO_4	3
Hydroxide	OH	1

All the compounds formed as a result of the electrovalent combination of an element with a radical are ionized (that is split into their ions) when they are dissolved in water, and they all fall into the category of either an *acid*, a *base*, or a *salt*. These three types of compound will now be mentioned separately.

Acids

Acids are formed by the electrovalent combination of hydrogen atoms and most radicals. The chief characteristic of acids is that in solution in water they yield hydrogen ions. The following equations give the formulae of the three principal mineral acids together with the ions they form when they are in solution in water:

Sulphuric acid	$H_2SO_4 \rightarrow 2H^+ + SO_4''$
Nitric acid	$HNO_3 \rightarrow H^+ + NO_3'$
Hydrochloric acid	$HCl \rightarrow H^+ + Cl'$

The $+$ sign indicates a positive ion, i.e. an atom which has lost one electron and therefore has a nuclear charge which is not balanced by an equal number of electrons.

The ′ sign indicates a negative ion, i.e. an atom or radical which has gained one electron more than is required to balance its nuclear charge.

The ″ sign indicates a doubly charged negative ion, i.e. an atom or radical which has gained two more electrons than it requires to balance its nuclear charge.

In the case of sulphuric acid, as the sulphate radical has a valency of 2, two hydrogen atoms are required to complete the stability of the group – hence the formula $H_{\textcircled{2}}SO_4$.

Nearly all acids are very corrosive to metals – an effect which is due to the facility with which metal atoms replace the hydrogen atoms of acids. A typical example is the reaction between zinc and sulphuric acid resulting in the formation of the salt zinc sulphate ($ZnSO_4$) thus:

$$Zn + H_2SO_4 \rightarrow ZnSO_4 + H_2$$

Alkalis and Bases

Alkalis are formed by the electrovalent combination of the hydroxide radical and most metals, or groups that behave as metals. The chief characteristic of an alkali is that in solution it will yield hydroxyl ions, as in the following typical cases:

Caustic soda (sodium hydroxide)	$NaOH \rightarrow Na^+ + OH'$
Caustic potash (potassium hydroxide)	$KOH \rightarrow K^+ + OH'$
Slaked lime (calcium hydroxide)	$Ca(OH)_2 \rightarrow Ca^+ + 2OH'$

In general this group of compounds may be extended to cover certain oxides, which, like the alkalis mentioned above, are able to neutralize acids; the word 'base' is used to include such oxides as well as hydroxides.

Salts

Salts are electrovalent compounds formed as the result of the neutralization of an acid by a base, a typical example being the formation of common salt, sodium chloride ($NaCl$), from sodium hydroxide and hydrochloric acid, thus:

$$NaOH + HCl \rightarrow NaCl + H_2O$$

or saltpetre, potassium nitrate (KNO_3), from potassium hydroxide and nitric acid, thus:

$$KOH + HNO_3 \rightarrow KNO_3 + H_2O$$

It will be noticed that in both the two examples above, the formation of the salt is accompanied by the formation of water: this is invariably the case and the definite rule may be stated that

$$\text{Acid} + \text{base} = \text{salt} + \text{water}$$

The formation of water results from the combination of the hydrogen and hydroxyl ions, thus:

$$H^+ + OH' \rightarrow H_2O$$

As we have already seen, this combination is covalent and consequently the water molecules once formed do not ionize, although there will always be a very small number of uncombined ions in equilibrium with the covalent molecules. Furthermore, we may also mention at this point that the covalent water molecules in the liquid state are *associated* together into loose complexes, so that a liquid water molecule should really be written $(H_2O)_n$. On heating to its boiling-point, however, liquid water *dissociates* and steam exists as single H_2O molecules.

OXIDATION AND REDUCTION

Apart from combining with certain elements to form radicals, oxygen, which is extremely reactive, will combine directly with most elements to form compounds called *oxides*, which we shall discuss shortly. The term 'oxidation', however, has a somewhat wider significance than denoting the formation of oxides, as it is used to describe both the addition of oxygen, or the removal of hydrogen from an element or compound.

The reverse of oxidation, that is the removal of oxygen, or the addition of hydrogen, is called *reduction*.

Oxides

As we have said, most elements form compounds with oxygen, indeed some elements form several different oxides. In general, the chemical properties of the different oxides depend upon the elements with which oxygen combines, so that several separate types of oxide can be distinguished. They are classified as follows:

BASIC OXIDES. These are compounds of oxygen and metals,

which react with acids to form salts. These oxides when dissolved in water form hydroxides (i.e. alkalis). For example, sodium oxide reacts with water to form sodium hydroxide:

$$Na_2O + H_2O \rightarrow 2NaOH$$

Basic oxides are always oxides of metals, and this fact is used as a definition of metals.

ACIDIC OXIDES. These are compounds of non-metals and oxygen which react with bases to form salts. An example is the gas carbon dioxide (CO_2), which reacts with sodium hydroxide (NaOH) to form the salt sodium carbonate:

$$CO_2 + 2NaOH \rightarrow Na_2CO_3 + H_2O$$

AMPHOTERIC OXIDES. Certain metallic oxides behave as both acidic and basic compounds, depending upon the circumstances; such oxides are said to be amphoteric. For example, aluminium trioxide (Al_2O_3) behaves as a base when reacted with hydrochloric acid to form aluminium chloride:

$$Al_2O_3 + 6HCl \rightarrow 2AlCl_3 + 3H_2O$$

Alternatively it will react with sodium hydroxide to form sodium aluminate ($NaAlO_2$), in which case it behaves as an acidic oxide:

$$Al_2O_3 + 2NaOH \rightarrow 2NaAlO_2 + H_2O$$

In addition to the three types of oxide mentioned above, there are also *neutral oxides*, *compound oxides*, and *peroxides*, but the details of these compounds need not worry us.

THE PERIODIC CLASSIFICATION OF THE ELEMENTS

In Chapter 2 we referred to the periodic table of the elements in which the ninety-two elements are classified according to their atomic numbers. We saw then that, by arranging the elements into nine vertical groups, each group was found to contain chemically similar elements as a result of similar configurations of their outer electrons. Before looking at each of these groups individually, it is interesting to look at the horizontal *periods* formed by this arrangement of the elements, and to note the development of chemical properties as we move across the periodic table from left to right.

Referring then to Table 3 (p. 54–5), it will be seen that, apart from the first horizontal line in which only hydrogen and helium appear, there are six periods. The first two periods are called short periods as they contain only one element per group, while the remaining four are called long periods because there are at least two elements in each group (except Group O).

In the first two short periods the properties of the twenty or so elements develop as each successive atom acquires an extra electron in its outer shell (see the diagram on page 32). In Group I the elements have only one electron in their outer shell, which they are able to donate quite readily in electrovalent combination, thus becoming positive ions. For this reason, these elements (which are called the *alkali metals*) are said to be *electropositive*. In general, the larger the atom, and therefore the farther the outer electrons from the nucleus, the easier it is for these valency electrons to be donated. Therefore the elements which are farthest down the group are the most electropositive.

At the other end of the table in Group VII, the elements have seven electrons in their outer shells, which makes them willing electron acceptors (it being remembered that all atoms strive to complete the octet of their outer electrons, see page 32). These elements are called the *halogens*, and as they form negative ions by acquiring an electron they are said to be *electronegative*. As we have already seen, strongly electropositive elements form electrovalent compounds with strongly electronegative elements (e.g., the formation of common salt, NaCl, sodium being an alkali metal and chlorine being a halogen).

In the first two periods of the table, then, there is a gradual change from the electropositive elements at one end to the electronegative elements at the other. In the middle are the elements of Group IV (carbon and silicon) which have four electrons in their outer shell, and which are neither willing donors nor acceptors of electrons. These elements therefore form covalent compounds.

After the two short periods comes the first long period which begins with the elements potassium and calcium. With these two

Table 3

THE PERIODIC CLASSIFICATION
OF THE ELEMENTS

I		II		III		IV		V	
A	B	A	B	A	B	A	B	A	B
3 Li			4 Be		5 B		6 C		7 N
11 Na		12 Mg		13 Al			14 Si		15 P
19 K		20 Ca		21 Sc		22 Ti		23 V	
	29 Cu		30 Zn		31 Ga		32 Ge		33 As
37 Rb		38 Sr		39 Y		40 Zr		41 Nb	
	47 Ag		48 Cd		49 In		50 Sn		51 Sb
55 Cs		56 Ba		57* La		72 Hf		73 Ta	
	79 Au		80 Hg		81 Tl		82 Pb		83 Bi
87 Fr		88 Ra		89† Ac					

* Lanthanons	57 La	58 Ce	59 Pr	60 Nd	61 Pm	62 Sm	63 Eu	64 Gd	65 Tb	66 Dy	67 Ho	68 Er	69 Tm	70 Yb	71 Lu
† Actinons	89 Ac	90 Th	91 Pa	92 U	93 Np	94 Pu	95 Am	96 Cm	97 Bk	98 Cf	99 E	100 Fm	101 Mv	102 No	

VI		VII		VIII			0
A	B	A	B				
		1 H					2 He
	8 O		9 F				10 Ne
	16 S		17 Cl				18 A
24 Cr		25 Mn		26 Fe	27 Co	28 Ni	
	34 Se		35 Br				36 Kr
42 Mo		43 Tc		44 Ru	45 Rh	46 Pd	
	52 Te		53 I				54 Xe
74 W		75 Re		76 Os	77 Ir	78 Pt	
	84 Po		85 At				86 Rn

elements the fourth electron shell is started, potassium having one electron in this shell and calcium two. Thereafter, however, the process changes as the fourth shell is stabilized with these two electrons, and subsequent electrons find their way back into the third shell. This procedure continues for ten elements until the third shell has expanded from eight to eighteen electrons; these ten elements are all metals, and as they all have only two electrons in their outer shell they all have similar properties. This is therefore an example of neighbours in the horizontal periods having similarities instead of the more usual similarities we have noted in the vertical groups.

Elements which have properties resembling those of their horizontal neighbours are called *transition elements*, but in general we may say that any element which has an incomplete *inner* shell is a transition element. Transition elements are characterized by having variable valencies, a property which they acquire as a result of the fact that under appropriate conditions electrons can be drawn from their penultimate shells into their outer shells where they become available for valency purposes.

After the transition elements in the first long period, added electrons continue to fill up the outer shell until this fourth shell is completed with eight electrons in the rare gas, krypton. We may therefore illustrate the growth of the electron shells in this period as in Figure 10.

	K	Ca	Sc	→ Zn	Ga	→ Kr
1st shell	2	2	2	2	2	2
2nd shell	8	8	8	8	8	8
3rd shell	8	8	9	18	18	18
4th shell	1	2	2	2	3	8
			(Transition Metals)			

Fig. 10

The second long period is very similar in structure to the first, as it also contains elements in which the number of electrons in the fourth shell increases from eight to eighteen, while the fifth shell builds up from one to eight, again finishing with a rare gas, in this case xenon. The transition metals in this period are similar to those in the first long period, so that in this part of the table similarities extend both horizontally and vertically.

The third long period is rather more complicated than its predecessors as it contains a group of fifteen elements called the *rare earths* or *lanthanons*, in which the fifth and sixth shells remain static with nine and two electrons respectively, while the fourth shell expands from eighteen to thirty-two electrons. Thereafter the fifth shell builds up to eighteen electrons and the sixth shell completes its octet with the radioactive rare gas, radon.

The lanthanons therefore form a special family of 'inner-transition' metals with chemical properties which are extremely similar. We can illustrate the build-up of electrons in this period in Figure 11.

	Cs	Ba	La →	Lu	Hf →	Hg	Tl →	Rn
1st shell	2	2	2	2	2	2	2	2
2nd shell	8	8	8	8	8	8	8	8
3rd shell	18	18	18	18	18	18	18	18
4th shell	18	18	18	32	32	32	32	32
5th shell	8	8	9	9	10	18	18	18
6th shell	1	2	2	2	2	2	3	8

← Transition metals →

Fig. 11

The fourth long period is again very similar to its predecessor except that the group parallel to the lanthanons, in this case called the *actinons*, is incomplete. Indeed, only the first six members of this period of elements (francium to uranium) are sufficiently stable to occur in nature; the remainder, from atomic number 93 upwards, are so highly radioactive, with such short half lives, that they can only be made artificially by nuclear reactions (which we shall discuss in Chapter 11). As the last naturally occurring element is uranium, the remaining members of the actinons are called *transuranic elements*.

It is hoped that this short description of the horizontal view of the periodic table will enable us to understand the properties of the elements which we find in the vertical groups.

The Sub-groups of the Periodic Table

As we saw in Chapter 2, after the two simple short periods, the vertical groups of the table have to be divided into two sub-groups designated A and B; from what has been said in the last few paragraphs, it should be clear that the reason for this expansion is the accommodation of the transition elements. It is also necessary, for the same reasons, to introduce an extra group (Group VIII) into the long periods, each with three transition metals per period. It is only in this way that the complications created by the transition elements can be resolved within the framework of the table.

In discussing the properties of the various elements, therefore, it will be necessary to distinguish between sub-groups A and B, and also to allocate the elements from the two short periods to the correct sub-group. This has been done in the presentation of the periodic table on pages 54–5.

Finally, before saying a few words about the elements of each group, we should note that in Group O, which contains the rare gases, no sub-groups are required as these elements stand quite apart from the rest of the table on account of their extremely stable structure.

GROUP I. In this group, unlike any of the other groups, the first two elements (lithium and sodium) closely resemble the elements of sub-group A rather than those of sub-group B. Furthermore, the elements comprising the two sub-groups are more dissimilar than those of the other groups; indeed, all they have in common is their univalency and the fact that they are all metals.

The first two elements and those of sub-group A are, as we have said, called the Alkali Metals – they are lithium, sodium, potassium, rubidium, and caesium. Of these elements by far the commonest are sodium and potassium which occur extensively in nature in the form of their salts (e.g., sodium chloride, sodium carbonate, potassium nitrate, etc.). In the uncombined metallic state, sodium and potassium are soft whitish substances which are extremely reactive. They both combine violently with water to form basic hydroxides, thus:

$$2Na + 2H_2O \rightarrow 2NaOH + H_2$$

The electropositive nature of these elements is shown by the properties of their salts, which are all freely soluble in water forming highly ionized solutions.

Sub-group B consists of the three 'noble' or 'coinage' metals, copper, silver, and gold, which are characterized by their high melting-points (all around 1,000°C) and the fact that they occur in nature in their uncombined metallic state, indicating that they are not very reactive.

The reason for their unreactivity, despite their single outer electron, is that their penultimate shells consist in all three cases of eighteen electrons, so that if the single outer electron were to be donated, the penultimate shell of eighteen electrons would become the outer shell. As eighteen electrons do not make a stable outer shell, and as reactions only occur if a more stable structure can be expected as a result of them, these elements do not readily form electrovalent compounds. However, under certain conditions, electrons from the penultimate shell can migrate to the outer shell, where they become available for valency purposes, and some salts can be formed. Thus copper sulphate ($CuSO_4$), in which copper has a valency of 2, is widely used as an insecticide, and the silver halides (silver bromide and silver iodide) are used in photographic emulsions.

GROUP II. In this group the first element, beryllium, resembles sub-group B, while the second element, magnesium, resembles the elements of sub-group A. All the elements in this group are exclusively divalent. Magnesium and the elements of sub-group A (calcium, strontium, barium, and radium) form a series of metals, called the *alkaline earths*, which are all strongly electropositive, though less so than the alkali metals. They are all very reactive and are therefore found in nature in the combined state.

Magnesium and calcium are the most common elements in this sub-group – magnesium occurring extensively in the form of its salts magnesium carbonate ($MgCO_3$, also known as dolomite) and magnesium sulphate ($MgSO_4$, also known as Epsom salts). Calcium carbonate occurs in vast quantities as chalk, and calcium sulphate also occurs widely in the earth's crust – being known as gypsum, alabaster, or plaster of Paris, depending upon the number of molecules of water contained in the crystals.

All the alkaline earths, as their name implies, form strongly basic oxides and hydroxides, as for example calcium oxide (CaO, known as quicklime) and calcium hydroxide ($Ca(OH)_2$, known as slaked lime). Radium, which is the last member of this group, is more important for its radioactive properties than for its chemical properties.

Sub-group B includes, as well as beryllium, the metals zinc, cadmium, and mercury. In general, zinc and cadmium show considerable similarities to calcium and magnesium. Mercury, however, is rather exceptional, being the only metal which is a liquid at normal temperature and pressure.

GROUP III. All the elements in this group are extremely scarce with the notable exception of aluminium which is, as we have seen, the third most common element on the surface of the earth, occurring very widely in the form of aluminium oxide (Al_2O_3, known as bauxite). Aluminium is a fairly reactive metal and readily forms an amphoteric oxide in air; it has a valency of 3, and most of its compounds are formed covalently. However, it forms an electrovalent compound with fluorine, and the commercial separation of the metal is carried out by the electrolysis (see page 140) of aluminium fluoride which is obtained by heating bauxite and a fusible fluoride.

Apart from aluminium, sub-group A includes the rare transition metals scandium and yttrium, as well as all the lanthanons and actinons. As we have already said, the lanthanons are all extremely rare, and interest in them has centred round their electronic structure and their place in the Periodic Table, rather than in their use. They do, however, form compounds, exhibiting, in addition to the group valency of 3, several other valencies on account of the migration of electrons from the penultimate to the outer shell.

The actinons are of importance because of their radioactive properties, which we shall be discussing together with their significance in the field of atomic energy in Chapter 11.

In sub-group B, boron is the only element which is sufficiently common to be of any interest. This element occurs in nature in combination with oxygen in the form of borates, notably sodium borate ($Na_2B_4O_7$, otherwise known as Borax). Its principal valency, like the other members of this group, is 3, and it forms covalent compounds (borides) with some metals.

The remaining members of this sub-group, gallium, indium, and thallium, are all transition metals with the principal valency of 3, which form covalent compounds.

GROUP IV. In this group, as in all the subsequent groups, the first two elements (carbon and silicon) are similar in character to the elements of sub-group B. However, these two elements are non-metals while the other members of the sub-group (germanium, tin, and lead) become progressively more metallic. Thus carbon in the form of diamond does not conduct electricity at all, but germanium is a semiconductor used in transistors, and tin and lead are typical metallic conductors.

As a result of having four electrons in their outer shells, the elements of this group have a principal valency of 4, which leads to the formation of stable covalent linkages. In addition, in the case of the first two elements, it permits the formation of very stable linkages between identical atoms. Indeed, life itself has been possible only because of the stability of the carbon-carbon bond, and the enormously large and complicated molecules that are formed as a result of it.

These, however, are aspects of carbon chemistry with which we shall deal in the next two chapters; here we need only mention that carbon and carbon compounds combine with oxygen, with the evolution of energy, to form the oxides carbon monoxide (CO) and carbon dioxide (CO_2). These reactions are the basis of combustion (see page 135) from which we obtain most of the energy for our civilization, for the fossil fuels (coal and oil) are predominantly carbon. Carbon dioxide is present in the earth's atmosphere to an extent of only about 0·03 per cent, but it is upon this small percentage that all life depends, for it is from atmospheric carbon dioxide that plants obtain their carbon by the process of photosynthesis (see page 105). As animals are dependent upon plants (and other animals) for their food, they too are therefore ultimately dependent for their carbon requirements upon atmospheric carbon dioxide.

The carbon removed in this way from the atmosphere is partly returned to it by respiration, and partly by the

liberation of carbon dioxide which attends the decomposition of
the dead bodies of plants and animals. Living matter thus main-
tains a remarkably steady percentage of carbon dioxide in the
atmosphere. Although most decomposing plant and animal
bodies liberate carbon dioxide into the atmosphere, a certain percentage of such decomposing matter finds its way below the
surface of the soil where it has to decay in the absence of oxygen –
over the ages this process has led to the formation of the fossil
fuels. The combustion of these fuels by man for the production
of energy is, as we have seen, again accompanied by the formation
of carbon dioxide which returns to the atmosphere.

In addition to these processes, atmospheric carbon dioxide is
absorbed by sea water, whence it is converted into the calcium
carbonate ($CaCO_3$) of the shells of aquatic animals. We may,
therefore, represent the natural carbon cycle as in Figure 12. The

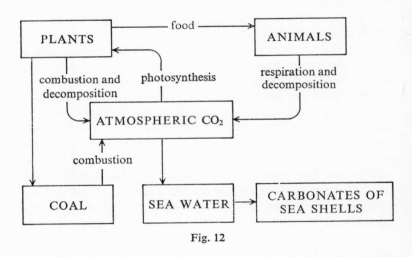

Fig. 12

other oxide of carbon, carbon monoxide, does not occur in
nature, but it is an important constituent of coal gas and is, of
course, extremely toxic.

The next element of this group is silicon, which is the second
most abundant element in the earth's crust, occurring principally
as silica (SiO_2) in the form of sand, flint, and quartz. Like carbon,

silicon atoms are also able to combine with other silicon atoms, but the Si—Si bond is considerably weaker than the C—C bond. For this reason the chemistry of silicon is much less extensive than that of carbon, although an interesting group of compounds called *silicones* have recently been artificially developed in imitation of the elementary organic carbon compounds.

Of the remaining elements of this sub-group not much need be said except that tin (stannous) compounds are more stable than germanium compounds and lead compounds are more stable still.

In sub-group A are found the elements titanium, zirconium, and hafnium, three transition metals with exceptionally high melting-points which combine actively with oxygen, nitrogen, and carbon. This property is made use of by adding small quantities of titanium and zirconium to steels with the object of increasing their mechanical strength by removing gaseous impurities trapped within the metal.

GROUP V. The first two elements of this group (nitrogen and phosphorus), and the elements of sub-group B (arsenic, antimony, and bismuth), form a graded series from the gaseous nitrogen to the metallic bismuth. Of these elements nitrogen and phosphorus are the most interesting, both being of great significance in the chemistry of life. Nitrogen, as we have already mentioned, is present in the earth's atmosphere to an extent of over 75 per cent, and although it is unreactive in the diatomic gaseous form, it will react with some metals at high temperatures and forms important compounds with hydrogen (ammonia, and ammonium salts) as well as with oxygen (oxides, nitrates, and nitrites).

In Chapter 6 we shall discuss the part played by nitrogenous organic compounds in biochemistry. All living matter acquires its nitrogen, like carbon, from plants, which in turn obtain it from the soil in the form of nitrates and ammonium salts. Again there is a cycle between living matter and the soil, as nitrates and ammonium salts are returned to the earth by the excretions of animals and the decomposition of plant and animal bodies. In this case the decomposition depends on the activities of bacteria in the soil which convert the organic matter into nitrates and free nitrogen which escapes into the atmosphere. A certain amount of atmospheric nitrogen is converted into ammonium nitrate by lightning and is washed back into the soil by rain. In addition some bacteria which live in the roots of certain leguminous plants are able to convert atmospheric nitrogen into nitrogenous foods for these plants. However, heavily cultivated soil does not obtain sufficient nitrogen in any of these ways and therefore nitrogen has to be added in the form of manure or artificial fertilizers. The general nitrogen cycle in nature can be illustrated as in Figure 13.

We have mentioned the compound ammonia (NH_3) which results from the covalent combination of one nitrogen atom with three hydrogen atoms; this compound is a gas, with a well-known pungent odour, which has the property of being able to collect an extra hydrogen ion forming the so-called ammonium ion NH_4^+. This ion forms electrovalent salts with the various radicals in much the same way as a metal and it is these salts which are used as fertilizers.

Phosphorus and the other elements of sub-group B also form volatile hydrides similar to ammonia, but they do not form stable ions capable of electrovalent combination. In Chapter 6 we shall see that phosphorus in the form of organic phosphates plays a vital part in the storing of energy by living organisms.

Sub-group A of Group V contains the rare transition metals vanadium, niobium, and tantalum, which are used in small quantities in steel alloys to confer the properties of high chemical resistance and stability at high temperatures.

GROUP VI. In this group the first two elements (oxygen and sulphur) form a series of non-metals with the elements of sub-group B (selenium, tellurium, and polonium), while sub-group A contains the transition metals chromium, molybdenum, and tungsten. These transition metals, however, are much more akin to the transition elements of sub-groups VA and VIIA than they are to sub-group B of Group VI.

Oxygen, as we have said, is the most common element on the surface of the earth, the atmosphere containing about 25 per cent of the diatomic gas and water containing nearly 90 per cent by weight of the combined element. Combined oxygen also occurs widely in the radicals of salts, as well as in oxides. Oxygen is highly reactive, combining in a number of ways with most

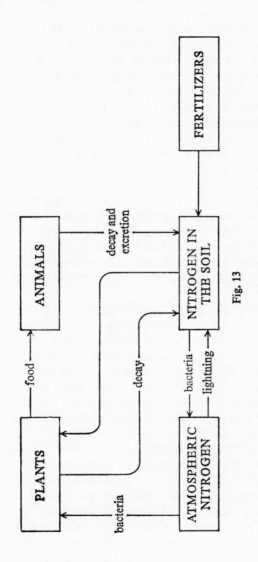

Fig. 13

3

elements – we have already given a brief description of the various types of oxides so formed.

Sulphur, like oxygen, has the group valency of 2, and forms a volatile hydride, hydrogen sulphide (H_2S), which is similar in construction to the hydride of oxygen, i.e. water. However, hydrogen sulphide is a gas at normal temperatures and pressures, and it is therefore surprising that water, which is after all a lighter molecule, should be a liquid. This is due to the association of water molecules which was mentioned on page 51.

Sulphur forms two common oxides, a dioxide (SO_2) and a trioxide (SO_3), both of which are gases. The dioxide dissolves in water to form sulphurous acid (H_2SO_3), the salts of which are called sulphites, while the trioxide dissolves in water to form sulphuric acid (H_2SO_4), the salts of which are called sulphates.

The transition metals of sub-group A are, as we have said, similar to their horizontal neighbours, exhibiting variable valencies, in most cases from 3 to 6. Again, due to their high melting-points and resistance to chemical attack, they are valuable for the properties they impart to steels with which they are alloyed.

GROUP VII. This group contains in its sub-group B the most electronegative of all the elements – the halogens (fluorine, chlorine, bromine, iodine, and astatine), while sub-group A contains the very dissimilar transition metals manganese, technetium, and rhenium. Of these elements two, astatine and technetium, do not occur in nature as they are too unstable, and they have only become known as a result of the transmutation of other elements.

The halogens have seven electrons in their outer shell, and being thus only one electron short of the rare-gas structure they are very reactive. The most reactive of all is fluorine, which will combine with most elements vigorously; although the other halogens behave similarly in this respect, they do so with decreasing vigour.

All the halogens form strong acids with hydrogen, hydrochloric acid, which we have already mentioned, being of wide industrial application. Hydrofluoric acid (HF) reacts with silicates and therefore attacks glass, and for this reason it has to be stored in either lead, plastic, or wax containers. Because of their ability to replace hydrogen atoms in covalent linkages, the halogens enter into many organic compounds, which we shall mention in the next chapter.

Of the sub-group A metals, only manganese is at all common in nature; it is a typical transition element showing all the valencies from 1 to 7 except 5, and again it is used as a constituent in both ferrous and non-ferrous alloys. The element hydrogen is often included in this group (as it has been in Table 3, p. 54), although it clearly fits into neither sub-group A nor B. In fact it has no well-defined position in the table as its solitary electron gives it a unique structure. It is, however, the simplest, the lightest, and the most abundant element in the universe, and, as we shall see in Chapter 12, all the other elements are made from it in the interior of certain stars. On the earth it occurs only to a tiny extent in the free state, although in the combined state it is very common as water contains over 10 per cent hydrogen by weight. Furthermore nearly all organic compounds contain hydrogen, as we shall see in the next chapter.

GROUP VIII. The nine transition metals contained in this group are rather difficult to treat comparatively although several ways have been devised of doing so. However, the first three, iron, cobalt, and nickel, differ from the other six metals in that they are much more reactive and rarely exhibit a greater valency than 3.

Iron is, for us, one of the most important elements which occurs on earth, as it has been the basic material of construction of our civilization. As it is readily oxidized it hardly ever occurs free in nature, but is widely distributed in the form of the ores haematite (Fe_2O_3) and magnetite (Fe_3O_4) from which the metal is obtained by reduction in a blast furnace. A very large proportion of the so-called 'pig-iron' produced by blast furnaces is converted into steel by the incorporation of a small quantity of carbon. As we have already mentioned, many of the other transition metals are also added to steels to give them special properties.

Iron forms two series of salts, the ferrous salts derived from ferrous oxide (FeO) and the ferric salts derived from ferric oxide (Fe_2O_3). Iron is unique in its magnetic properties, although cobalt and nickel are both slightly magnetic. It is considerably more reactive than either cobalt or nickel, both of which are added to special steels in order to confer the properties of resistance to chemical attack, particularly oxidation.

The other six metals in the group (ruthenium, rhodium, palladium, osmium, iridium, and platinum) are often known collectively as the 'platinum metals'; they are all extremely rare and unreactive. Platinum and palladium are widely used as industrial catalysts (substances which increase the speed of chemical reactions without actually taking part in them; see page 100).

GROUP O. As we have already said, the rare gases have complete octets of outer electrons and therefore form no compounds; consequently they have no chemistry.

These gases are all found to a small extent in the earth's atmosphere, the commonest, argon, being present to an extent of nearly 1 per cent. As we shall see in Chapter 12, helium is present in the sun as a result of thermonuclear reactions. All these gases are of industrial use on account of their unreactivity and are used for filling electric lamps and providing a non-reactive atmosphere for welding oxidizable metals.

CHAPTER 5

ORGANIC MATTER

In the last chapter, it was mentioned that Group IV of the periodic table contains the element carbon which, owing to its valency of 4, has the remarkable property of combining with itself as well as with other elements, so that it is able to produce very large molecules.

Organic chemistry is the study of such compounds of carbon. At the beginning of the section on matter, it was stated that organic chemistry is the study of matter from which living things are, or have been, made, and this is so because nearly all matter that is, or has been, living consists of compounds of the element carbon. In fact, it is the ability of carbon to combine with itself and form large molecules that has made life possible – such considerations, however, belong to biochemistry (Chapter 6).

It must be added, here, that modern organic chemistry has been extended to cover the study of such man-made materials as synthetic resins and fibres. While it is true that these compounds are manufactured in factories and laboratories, and are not 'organic' in the sense that they are made by natural processes, they are all derived from coal, oil, or other fossil, animal, or vegetable products.

Organic compounds are divided into two main groups, depending on their structure, namely:

1. *Aliphatic* or straight-chain molecules
2. *Cyclic* or ring-shaped molecules

In the more complicated large organic compounds a combination of both types is quite common. Each of the above two main groups can be subdivided into smaller groups as will be seen from the following outline.

ALIPHATIC COMPOUNDS

Aliphatic compounds are subdivided into three principal types, all of which are based on covalent bonds (see page 34) between the carbon atoms, but in each type the number of such bonds differs, as will be explained below. The three types of aliphatic compounds are:

1. The paraffins.
2. The olefins.
3. The acetylenes.

Each type must now be described separately.

THE PARAFFINS. In all these compounds the atoms are linked to each other by single covalent bonds, as in Figure 14. This compound is called *methane* (marsh gas), and has the formula CH_4.

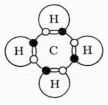

Fig. 14

As the covalent bond is extremely common in organic chemistry, for simplicity it is usual to depict a covalent pair of shared electrons as a single line, so that the methane molecule is usually written:

$$\begin{array}{c} H \\ | \\ H-C-H \\ | \\ H \end{array}$$

This molecule, methane, is the first and the simplest member of a whole series of paraffin molecules of increasing size. Each member of the series is called a *homologue*, and each homologue is formed by replacing one hydrogen atom with an additional carbon atom. Thus the second member of the series, ethane (C_2H_6), is constructed as follows:

$$\begin{array}{cc} H & H \\ | & | \\ H-C-C-H \\ | & | \\ H & H \end{array}$$

As each carbon atom has a valency of 4, six hydrogen atoms, each providing one electron, are required to complete the octets of both carbon atoms.

The next member of the series, propane, formula C_3H_8, has three carbon atoms:

$$
\begin{array}{ccccccc}
 & H & & H & & H & \\
 & | & & | & & | & \\
H- & C & - & C & - & C & -H \\
 & | & & | & & | & \\
 & H & & H & & H &
\end{array}
$$

In this and subsequent members of the series the inner carbon atoms require only two hydrogen atoms as they are linked on each side with other carbon atoms. It will be realized that an almost indefinite series of compounds can be built up in this way, with a general formula C_nH_{2n+2}. As the chain becomes larger, the molecules become heavier and consequently the higher homologues are liquids and higher still they become solids. The following table gives the commonest members of this group and their physical state at normal temperatures and pressures:

Methane	CH_4	gas
Ethane	C_2H_6	gas
Propane	C_3H_8	gas
Butane	C_4H_{10}	gas
Pentane	C_5H_{12}	liquid
Hexane	C_6H_{14}	liquid
Heptane	C_7H_{16}	liquid
Octane	C_8H_{18}	liquid
Hexadecane	$C_{16}H_{34}$	solid

The paraffins exist in nature as the main constituents of petroleum. The refining process separates the heavier from the lighter members of the series. For example, petrol (gasoline) consists mostly of pentane, hexane, and octane, whereas kerosene contains mixtures of the various compounds from $C_{10}H_{22}$ to $C_{16}H_{34}$. The natural gas that is often found with oil, but sometimes alone, is itself used as a fuel, and consists of a mixture of the first four members of the series.

Isomerism

It will be realized that from the fourth member of the series onwards, more than one form of each molecule can exist, as will be seen from the following structural formulae:

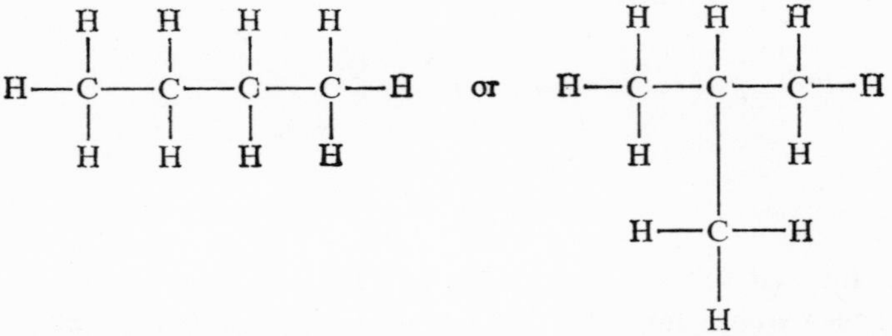

Normal butane   Iso-Butane

When a compound can exist in more than one form in this way, the various forms are called *isomers* and the compound is said to be *isomeric*. Branching of the chains in such molecules can obviously occur more frequently in the higher homologues. For example $C_{10}H_{22}$ could have 159 isomers, although only two are known to exist. In many cases isomers have different properties from each other.

Properties of the Paraffins and the Halogens

The Paraffin Series of compounds are called *saturated compounds* because the carbon atoms have combined with the maximum number of hydrogen atoms, and for this reason this type of compound is relatively unreactive. However, the hydrogen atoms can be replaced quite easily with atoms of the halogen group of elements. For example, in the case of methane, one, two, three, or all of the hydrogen atoms can be replaced by chlorine, forming the following compounds:

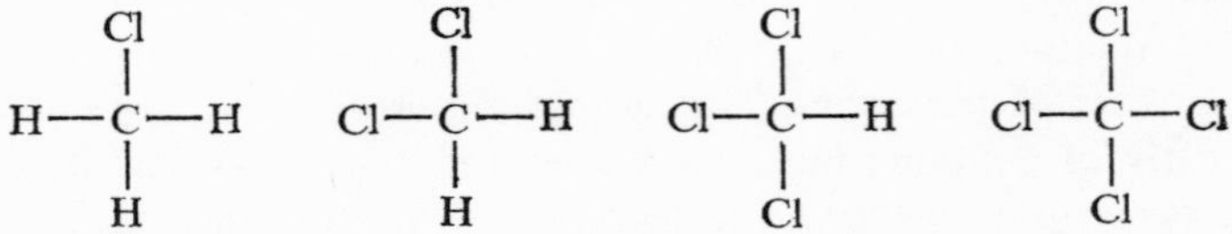

methyl chloride   dichloro-methane   chloroform   carbon
CH_3Cl CH_2Cl_2 $CHCl_3$ tetrachloride
                                                         CCl_4

Similar compounds can be formed with iodine, bromine, and fluorine with all other members of the series.

THE OLEFINS. The second type of aliphatic series is based on a double covalent linkage between the carbon atoms. The first member of this series contains two carbon atoms and is called ethylene C_2H_4. Using the same symbols as before for the electron pairs, this molecule is usually written: $CH_2=CH_2$. These compounds are called *unsaturated*, and as a result of their double bond they are able to take a further two atoms of hydrogen into their molecule. Consequently they are considerably more reactive than the paraffins.

The subsequent members of the series, which have a general formula C_nH_{2n}, exist either with their double bonds separated by two or more single bonds, as, for example:

$$
\begin{array}{ccccc}
\text{H} & \text{H} & \text{H} & \text{H} & \text{H} \\
| & | & | & | & | \\
\text{H}-\text{C}=\text{C}-\text{C}-\text{C}=\text{C} \\
& & | & & | \\
& & \text{H} & & \text{H}
\end{array}
$$

or with the double bonds separated by only one single bond:

$$C=C-C=C-C$$

This second isomer is said to have a conjugated double bond. *Butadiene*, which is the basis of synthetic rubber, has a conjugated double bond as will be seen from its formula:

$$CH_2=CH-CH=CH_2.$$

The olefins may also have hydrogen atoms substituted by halogen atoms, in the same way as the paraffins. The compound vinyl chloride is simply ethylene with one hydrogen atom replaced with a chlorine atom: $CH_2=CH.Cl$.

As a result of their double bond many single molecules can be made to link up together forming a long chain. This process is known as *polymerization* and in the case of vinyl chloride the resulting polymer is the well-known plastic, polyvinyl chloride (PVC). The substance before it has polymerized is called a *monomer* (see p. 86).

THE ACETYLENES. The third series of aliphatic compounds is

based on two carbon atoms attached to each other by a triple covalent bond. The first member of the series, and the only one of any importance, is acetylene (C_2H_2), which has the structure:

$$H - C \equiv C - H$$

Acetylene is a gas, obtained by adding water to calcium carbide, and is extensively used in the manufacture of organic compounds. It is also used for welding owing to the very hot flame it produces when burnt in oxygen.

If acetylene is passed through a red-hot tube, the triple bond breaks down and three molecules join together into a stable ring-compound called benzene, C_6H_6, with the structure:

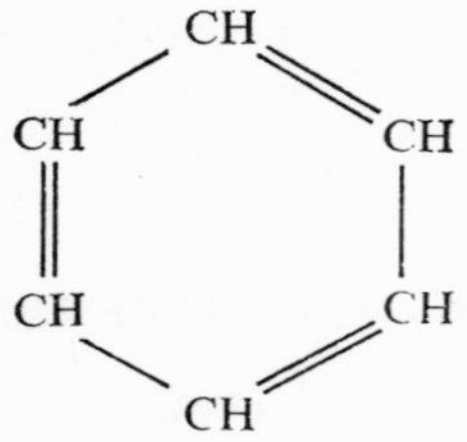

This compound is the basis of all the cyclic molecules which are described on page 80. The acetylenes have the general formula C_nH_{2n-2}.

Substituted Aliphatic Compounds

All the aliphatic compounds are able to form *substitution products*, in which one or more of the hydrogen atoms are replaced by other groups of atoms. Some substitution products involving halogen atoms have already been mentioned; other such compounds will now be described.

As many compounds are formed by the substitution of only one hydrogen atom from the molecule, it is convenient to regard the groups $-CH_3$, $-C_2H_5$, $-C_3H_7$, etc., as *radicals* of the Paraffin Series. Similarly the group $CH_2=CH-$ is the vinyl radical of the Olefin Series, and the group $CH\equiv C-$ is the acetyl radical of the Acetylene Series.

These organic radicals are covalently bonded to the groups or atoms with which they form compounds and not electrovalently as with inorganic radicals.

Alcohols

One of the most important groups of compounds results from the substitution of hydrogen atoms in organic compounds by the *hydroxyl group* —OH. All organic compounds which contain this hydroxyl group are called *alcohols*. They differ from inorganic compounds which contain the —OH group in that the method of bonding is covalent and not electrovalent, and consequently alcohols do not ionize in solution and are not bases.

Each member of the Paraffin Series forms an alcohol, and the name of each alcohol follows the name of the paraffin which contains the same number of carbon atoms. The first and commonest members of the series are:

Methyl alcohol (CH_3—OH), also called methanol or wood spirit.
Ethyl alcohol (C_2H_5—OH), also called ethanol (the intoxicant in alcoholic drinks).
Propyl alcohol (C_3H_7—OH), also called propanol.
Butyl alcohol (C_4H_9—OH), also called butanol.

Although the olefins and acetylenes also form alcohols, they are not of great industrial importance.

The alcohols mentioned so far contain only one —OH group in the molecule; several important compounds exist, however, in which more than one hydrogen atom is replaced by a hydroxyl group. The commonest compound, derived from propane, is glycerine or glycerol, which has three hydroxyl groups, arranged as in the following structural formula:

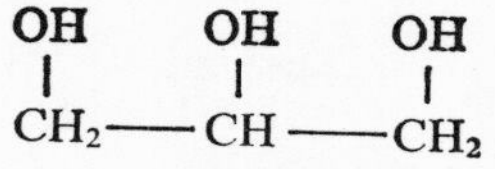

$$\begin{array}{ccc} OH & OH & OH \\ | & | & | \\ CH_2 \!\!-\!\!\!-\!\! CH \!\!-\!\!\!-\!\! CH_2 \end{array}$$

Compounds containing more than one hydroxyl group are called *poly-hydric* alcohols.

If an alcohol is reacted with an inorganic acid, the compound formed is called an *inorganic ester*. Typical of such compounds is methyl nitrate, which is formed from methyl alcohol thus:

$$CH_3OH \quad + \quad HNO_3 \quad \rightarrow \quad CH_3ONO_2 \quad + H_2O$$

Methyl alcohol   Nitric acid   Methyl nitrate   Water

If glycerine is reacted with nitric acid in this way so that all three hydroxyl groups are nitrated, the resulting compound is called *tri-nitro-glycerine*, the explosive in dynamite.

Ethers

Another group of compounds of importance can be formed by allowing two molecules of alcohol to react together under certain conditions, so that a molecule of water is removed. For example:

$$C_2H_5-O!H + OH!-C_2H_5 \quad \longrightarrow C_2H_5-O-C_2H_5 \quad + H_2O$$

ethyl alcohol   di-ethyl ether   water

This type of reaction, in which a molecule of water is removed, is called a *condensation reaction*. In this particular condensation reaction the product is called an *ether*, and in the example given the compound formed is *di-ethyl ether* (the anaesthetic commonly known as 'ether'). Similar compounds may be formed from other alcohols; for example, if a molecule of methyl alcohol is reacted with a molecule of propyl alcohol the resulting compound is called methyl-propyl ether.

Carboxylic or Fatty Acids

These acids result from the oxidation of alcohols. It is a common experience that wine left open to the air becomes sour and vinegary. This is due to the oxidation of ethyl alcohol to acetic acid (the main constituent of vinegar) which can be represented thus:

ethyl alcohol   becomes   acetic acid

All compounds which contain the carboxyl group

are called *carboxylic* or *fatty acids*. Their acidity is due to the fact that in solution the carboxyl group ionizes, liberating hydrogen ions.

The commonest fatty acids are given below:

H.COOH – Formic acid made from methyl alcohol.
CH_3COOH – Acetic acid made from ethyl alcohol.
C_2H_5COOH – Propionic acid made from propyl alcohol.
C_3H_7COOH – Butyric acid made from butyl alcohol.

The alcohols of olefins also form similar acids, an important example being acrylic acid, which is used in the plastics industry and has the formula $CH_2{=}CH.COOH$. This compound forms the well-known plastic methyl methacrylate (see p. 87).

Fatty acids form salts with inorganic alkalis in a similar manner to inorganic acids. For example, acetic acid and sodium hydroxide react together to form the salt sodium acetate and water, thus:

$$CH_3COOH \quad + \quad NaOH \quad \rightarrow \quad CH_3COONa + H_2O$$
Acetic acid   sodium hydroxide   Sodium acetate   Water

These compounds ionize in water as the sodium atom is bonded electrovalently to the acetate radical; they are therefore true salts.

If a fatty acid is reacted with an alcohol, a covalent compound called an *organic ester* is formed which does not ionize. A typical example is the formation of the ester, ethyl acetate, from ethyl alcohol and acetic acid:

$$CH_3COOH \quad + \quad C_2H_5OH \quad \rightarrow \quad CH_3COOC_2H_5 + H_2O$$
Acetic acid   Ethyl alcohol   Ethyl acetate   Water

This is another example of a condensation reaction. Ethyl acetate is a liquid which is widely used in industry as a solvent. Higher esters are solid compounds; fats are the esters of glycerine and waxes are even higher complex esters. In general, animal fats are saturated esters, while vegetable fats are unsaturated esters.

Aldehydes

If an alcohol is dehydrogenated, that is has certain atoms of hydrogen removed, the hydroxyl group breaks up and the group

—CHO is formed. All compounds containing this group are called *aldehydes*. The formation of aldehydes from alcohols can be illustrated as follows:

$$H—\overset{\displaystyle H}{\underset{\displaystyle H}{C}}—O\,H \quad\text{becomes}\quad H—\underset{\displaystyle H}{C}\!=\!O \;+\; H_2$$

methyl alcohol   formaldehyde   hydrogen

Formaldehyde ('formalin') the first in the series of aldehydes, is used as a disinfectant and for preserving medical specimens. The second member of the series is called acetaldehyde (CH_3CHO), and is made from ethyl alcohol.

If aldehydes are oxidized they form fatty acids, and the names of the aldehydes are derived from the acids they form, not the alcohols from which they are made:

	$-H_2$ forms		$+O$ forms	
CH_3OH methyl alcohol	$\longrightarrow$	H.CHO formaldehyde	$\longrightarrow$	H.COOH formic acid
C_2H_5OH ethyl alcohol	$\longrightarrow$	CH_3CHO acetaldehyde	$\longrightarrow$	CH_3COOH acetic acid
C_3H_7OH propyl alcohol	$\longrightarrow$	C_2H_5CHO propaldehyde	$\longrightarrow$	C_2H_5COOH propionic acid

Ketones

The structure of the *ketones* is somewhat similar to that of the aldehydes, except that the hydrogen atom in the aldehyde group —CHO is replaced by a second organic radical, as for example in the first member of the series, dimethyl ketone:

$$CH_3—C\!\!\underset{\displaystyle O}{\overset{\displaystyle CH_3}{\diagup}}$$

This compound is better known as acetone and is widely used in industry as a solvent. A whole series of ketones can be formed, which like the ethers may contain mixed groups of radicals, as for example methyl-ethyl ketone.

Amines

If alcohols are reacted with the gas ammonia, a group of compounds called *amines* are formed by condensation:

$$CH_3OH + NH_3 \rightarrow CH_3NH_2 + H_2O$$

Methyl   Ammonia   Methylamine   Water
alcohol

This compound methylamine is a primary amine and is used as a refrigerant. Secondary and tertiary amines can also be formed as illustrated by the formulae:

di-methylamine $\quad \begin{array}{c} CH_3 \\ \\ CH_3 \end{array}\!\!\!\!\!>\!NH \quad$ written $\quad (CH_3)_2NH$

tri-methylamine $\quad \begin{array}{c} CH_3 \\ CH_3 \\ CH_3 \end{array}\!\!\!\!\!>\!N \quad$ written $\quad N(CH_3)_3$

Ammonia can also be made to react with the hydrogen atoms in the radical part of an alcohol molecule, as for example in ethanolamine, NH_2—C_2H_4—OH. Similarly, the tertiary compound tri-ethanolamine, $(C_2H_4OH)_3N$, can be formed. This compound is a useful solvent in the paint industry.

Summary of Aliphatic Compounds

As several types of compound have been described a summary of their general form will probably be of use. Using the symbols R and R' to represent any organic radicals, the following compounds can be made:

R—OH	an alcohol.
R—ONO$_2$	an inorganic ester.
R—O—R'	an ether.
R—COOH	a fatty acid.
R—COONa	the salt of a fatty acid.
R—COOR'	an organic ester.
R—CHO	an aldehyde.
R—CO—R'	a ketone.
R—NH$_2$	an amine.

CYCLIC COMPOUNDS

Cyclic carbon compounds are groups in which the carbon and hydrogen atoms arrange themselves into a ring-structure. The main group of cyclic compounds are the so-called *aromatics* which are based on the ring compound benzene, C_6H_6.

It was stated in dealing with the acetylenes that if the gas acetylene is passed through a red-hot tube, a six-carbon ring-compound is formed with alternate double bonds. This has the structural formula:

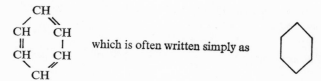

This compound, benzene, is present in the distillation products of coal tar and is the basis of very many useful products.

Coal Tar

When coal is gasified in a gas-works to produce the gas with which we cook, the products of gasification are:

A *gas*, consisting of carbon monoxide, hydrogen, nitrogen, methane, and ethylene which is used as town gas;

A *liquid* consisting of water and ammonia;

Coal tar which is a viscous tar consisting of pitch, benzene, naphthalene, anthracene, cresols, and other cyclic compounds;

A *solid* – coke.

Coal tar is the source of nearly all the aromatic compounds and their derivatives which will be described in the following paragraphs.

Despite the presence of double bonds in aromatic compounds, they do not behave as unsaturated compounds and are quite stable. Nevertheless, the hydrogen atoms can be replaced by other organic radicals, and the group C_6H_5—, called the *phenyl group*, can itself be considered as a radical, as for example in the compound phenyl chloride, formula $C_6H_5.Cl$. Some important combinations of benzene with other radicals will now be described.

TOLUENE – $C_6H_5 \cdot CH_3$. This is the first derivative of benzene in which one hydrogen atom is replaced by a methyl group:

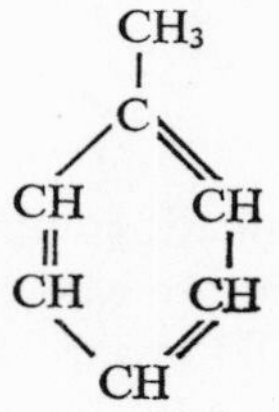

$$
\begin{array}{c}
CH_3 \\
| \\
C \\
CH \qquad CH \\
CH \qquad CH \\
CH
\end{array}
$$

If this compound is treated with nitric acid it becomes nitrated forming mono-, di-, and tri-nitrotoluene. The last-named compound is well known as the explosive TNT.

ANILINE – $C_6H_5 \cdot NH_2$. In this compound one hydrogen atom of the benzene ring is replaced with an amine group:

$$
NH_2
$$

Aniline is the basis of many dyes and drugs. If aniline is reacted with sulphuric acid in a certain way, the sulphanilamide group of drugs are produced. The formula of sulphanilamide is:

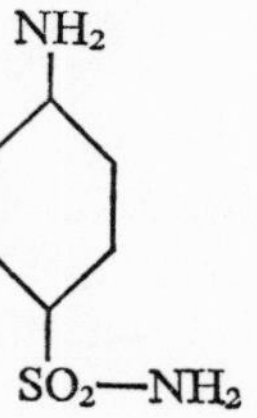

$$
NH_2
$$
$$
SO_2—NH_2
$$

PHENOL – $C_6H_5 \cdot OH$. This compound, also known as carbolic acid, is produced by the replacement of one hydrogen atom of the benzene ring by a hydroxyl group:

OH

This compound, unlike aliphatic compounds containing an—OH group, is not an alcohol but an acid, owing to the fact that the hydrogen atom of the —OH group is electrovalently combined with the rest of the molecule. Phenol is widely used as an antiseptic.

CYCLIC CARBOXYLIC ACIDS. The simplest such compound, benzoic acid, $C_6H_5 \cdot COOH$, is formed by the addition of the fatty acid group —COOH to the benzene ring, thus:

COOH

If the carboxyl group is added to phenol, an acid called salicylic acid is formed with the structure:

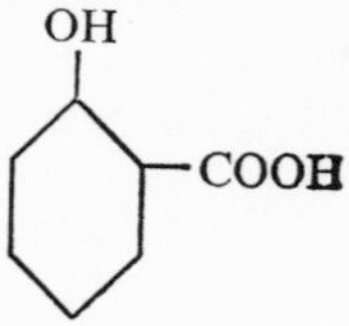

OH

—COOH

This compound is the basis of aspirin.

If two carboxyl groups are added to a benzene ring the resulting compound is phthalic acid, with the formula:

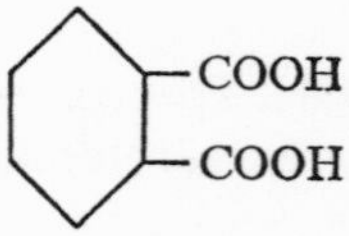

—COOH
—COOH

NAPHTHALENE, $C_{10}H_8$. This compound, which is present in coal tar, is formed by the joining together of two benzene rings:

$$
\begin{array}{ccc}
& \text{CH} & \text{CH} \\
\diagup & \diagdown \diagup & \diagdown \\
\text{CH} & \text{C} & \text{CH} \\
\parallel & | & | \\
\text{CH} & \text{C} & \text{CH} \\
\diagdown & \diagup \diagdown & \diagup \\
& \text{CH} & \text{CH}
\end{array}
$$

Naphthalene is itself well known for its use in moth-balls. It forms many derivatives in exactly the same way as benzene, and it is widely used in the dyestuffs industry.

SYNTHETIC RESINS AND FIBRES

Broadly speaking, it has been the need for a raw material capable of being easily and cheaply moulded into serviceable domestic articles that has led to the development of the synthetic-resin or 'plastics' industry. Although certain substances which occur in nature have been used in the past for these purposes, such as horn and shellac, they are relatively rare and expensive, and for some uses may have undesirable chemical or physical properties. Thus the search for a substitute for natural horn led to the discovery of Celluloid, while Bakelite was the outcome of an attempt to replace shellac. Synthetic resins, then, are amorphous substances manufactured by man, chiefly from the by-products of coal gasification and oil refining, which have the property of becoming plastic on heating. They can therefore be moulded into any desired shape, quickly and cheaply, in high-pressure heated moulding presses.

Resins which can only be used once in this way are said to be *thermosetting,* as once 'set' under heat they never regain their plasticity, while those which can be repeatedly remoulded by heating are said to be *thermoplastic.* It will be convenient to discuss the principal resins in common use under these two headings.

Thermosetting Resins

All synthetic resins are, as we have said, amorphous solids comprising large molecules based on carbon. By describing one of these substances, Bakelite, we shall see how thermosetting resins are formed, and how they differ in structure from thermoplastics. The first stage in the manufacture of Bakelite consists of condensing phenol ($C_6H_5.OH$) and formaldehyde ($H.CHO$) molecules together to form long chains:

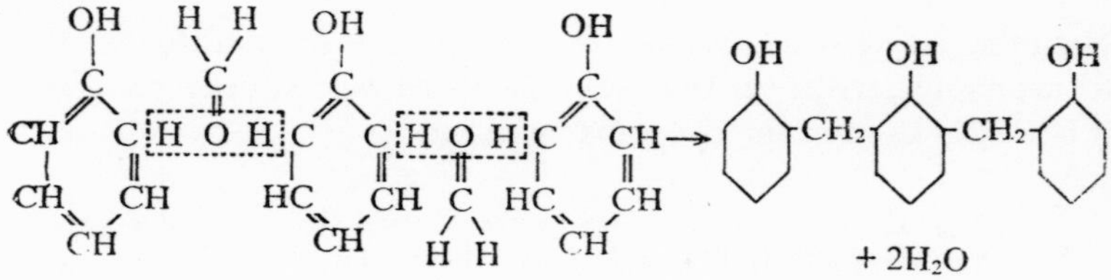

The chain illustrated here only includes three phenol molecules, but in practice very long chains are formed giving a liquid resinous substance. On standing, however, cross-linkages occur between the chains, so that a solid structure develops, thus:

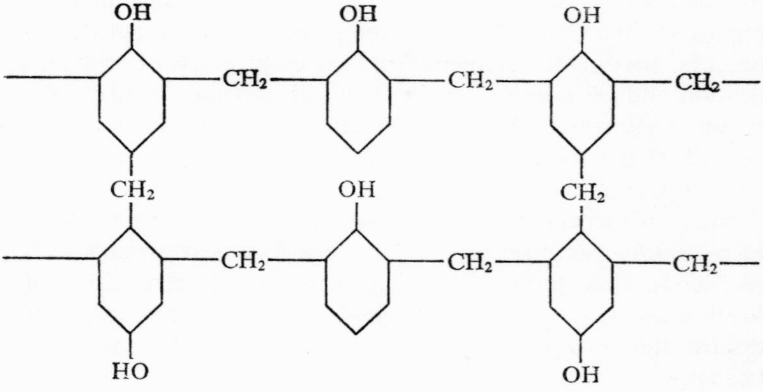

This is only a two-dimensional model, but in fact cross-linkages develop in three dimensions so that a 'honeycomb' network is formed. It is the cross-linkages of these true chemical bonds which give the thermosetting resins their strength and their resistance to heat, whereas the thermoplastics, as we shall see, have to rely upon the weaker molecular forces between their long-chain molecules.

A similar group to the phenol-formaldehyde resins are the amino-plastics, of which the most common are formed from the condensation of urea, $CO(NH_2)_2$, and formaldehyde molecules. These resins are used for light-coloured articles such as plastic tea-cups, for which the dark-coloured phenol-formaldehyde resins are unsuitable.

Another thermosetting resin, which is also used as a synthetic fibre, is nylon, which has been built up by organic chemists in imitation of natural silk. In attempting to produce a synthetic material with greater strength than silk, which is a protein consisting of chains of amino acids linked together in a polypeptide chain (see page 101), a group of substances have been evolved, called *super polyamides*, in which fatty acids are condensed with amides. Nylon itself is formed by the condensation of adipic acid,

$$COOH—(CH_2)_4—COOH$$

and hexamethylene diamine,

$$NH_2—(CH_2)_6—NH_2$$

with the result that a chain is formed thus:

$$—NH—(CH_2)_6—NH—CO—(CH_2)_4—CO—$$

Nylon is used as a plastic as well as a fibre, and in the latter form it can be drawn into threads which are stronger, finer, and more resistant to chemical attack than natural silk.

We have mentioned only a few of the thermosetting resins – there are of course others with many interesting uses – but, as it is not our purpose to give an exhaustive list of all these products, we shall pass on to describe a few of the most prominent thermoplastics.

Thermoplastics

As we have already said, thermoplastics differ from thermosetting resins in that their chains are not cross-linked with chemical bonds. At normal temperatures the molecules of thermoplastics are held together as amorphous solids only by molecular forces (see page 42), which at elevated temperatures are insufficiently strong to prevent the molecules from slipping over each other. It is for this reason that such substances become plastic whenever they are heated. In general, while we have seen that thermosetting resins are the result of condensation reactions, thermoplastics are the result of polymerization reactions.

The earliest synthetic resin of all, Celluloid, and its more modern derivatives, are thermoplastics based on naturally occurring cellulose obtained mostly from cotton. Natural cellulose, as we shall see in the next chapter (page 108), is made up of chains of glucose units, and it is these chains which form the basis of all the cellulose plastics.

Celluloid is made by mixing camphor with cellulose which has been nitrated (a hydroxyl group replaced by a $-NO_2$ group). The disadvantage of this material is that it is highly inflammable; however, this difficulty has been overcome in the more modern derivative, cellulose acetate. In this case the hydroxyl group is not nitrated but is substituted by an acetyl ($CH_3 \cdot COO-$) group. Rayon, a form of artificial silk, is made from cellulose acetate.

Other important thermoplastics are the polystyrenes and the polyvinyls. Styrene is an unsaturated phenyl derivative of ethylene with the structure:

$$CH=CH_2$$

This compound, which is a by-product of the oil industry, can be made to polymerize in the presence of certain catalysts, into a long-chain molecule giving a clear glass-like resin which is widely used in the radio and electrical industries. Similarly, vinyl resins are polymers of the vinyl group $CH_2=CH-$, the most common ones in use being polyvinyl chloride (PVC), $CH_2=CH.Cl$, and polyvinyl acetate (PVA), $CH_2=CH.OOC.CH_3$. These two molecules can be made to polymerize together, and, in addition to their separate uses, the so-called co-polymer of PVC and PVA has its own valuable properties and uses.

Another well-known resin of this type, based on the methyl ester of methacrylic acid ($CH_2\!=\!C(CH_3)\!-\!COOH$), is methyl methacrylate which has the formula: $CH_2\!=\!C(CH_3)\!-\!COOCH_3$. This polymer, which is sold under the names of Perspex, Plexiglas, and Lucite, has valuable optical properties which has led to its use in the moulding of cheap lenses.

No survey of plastic materials, however brief, would be complete without mentioning casein, with properties falling between the thermoplastic and the thermosetting. This material is a protein found in milk in combination with calcium. The calcium caseinogenate is separated from the milk by using a coagulant such as rennet; the casein so obtained is dried, finely ground, and moulded by a press into the desired shape. Up to this stage it is a thermoplastic, but thereafter it is hardened into a thermosetting compound by the action of formaldehyde. Casein is widely used in knife handles, buttons, fountain-pen cases, etc.

CHAPTER 6

LIVING MATTER

HAVING described the chemical nature of inanimate matter in some detail, we are now able to examine the chemistry of living matter. This study constitutes the subject of biochemistry, though the broader field, dealing with the classification and development of living organisms, is called biology. In this chapter, then, some of what we shall say properly belongs to biology and some to biochemistry: the boundary between the two subjects is not clear-cut.

LIFE

It is not known exactly when life first made its appearance on our planet, but it is estimated as being between 500 million and 3,000 million years ago, as compared to an estimated age of the earth of at least 4,000 million years. Nor is it known whether life first appeared in one place on the surface of the earth at one particular instant of time, or whether it was spontaneously created at various places and at various times. We are, however, fairly certain that new life is not *now* being spontaneously created from inanimate matter – a subject we shall refer to again in our final chapter. As regards the distinction between that which is animate and that which is not, again we are unable to be rigid: as we shall see when we come to mention viruses, the difference is not as clear as it might at first seem to be. Nevertheless, as a working hypothesis, it is generally agreed amongst biologists and biochemists that living matter is characterized by the following properties:

Reproduction – the ability to create a new generation.
Respiration – the ability to use the oxygen of the atmosphere for the production of energy by combustion.
Nutrition – the ability to obtain from the surroundings the materials required for growth and reproduction.

Excretion – the ability to dispose of waste products.

Irritability – the ability to respond to such external stimuli as heat, light, etc.

These characteristics may be summarized by saying that a living organism is self-replicating and self-regulating.

The Cell

Life, like matter itself, is quantized, that is to say there is a minimum unit of matter which can be said, according to the above definition, to be living. This unit is called a *cell* – an entity which we shall have to examine in some detail.

Before doing so, however, it must be admitted that there is a great deal about the reactions which occur inside cells which we do not understand. Indeed, one fact stands out very clearly – the matter from which life is constructed, called in general *protoplasm*, is extremely complex. Whereas the largest inanimate molecules consist of either relatively few atoms or chains of many atoms which repeat the same simple structure over and over again, protoplasm contains very large numbers of atoms arranged in an orderly but non-repetitive manner. As we shall see later, the structure of the simplest proteins is only now beginning to be unravelled. One of the secrets of life then, perhaps *the* secret, is its ordered complexity; this is a point which we shall return to again.

For the present we must concentrate on the cells themselves, of which, we have said, all living things are made; the simplest and most primitive life-forms consist of only one cell, while more developed organisms are made up of large numbers. A man, for instance, consists of millions of different cells performing a variety of different functions.

A cell, which may be between a tenth and a hundredth of a millimetre in diameter (there are exceptions both in shape and size), usually has two distinct forms of protoplasm – the *cytoplasm* and within the cytoplasm the *nucleus*. These two parts of the cell must now be described separately.

THE NUCLEUS. First, the nucleus of a cell must not be confused with the nucleus of an atom; it is unfortunate that the same word is used to describe these two different entities.

The nucleus of a cell in the resting stage (i.e. when it is not reproducing itself), is separated from the cytoplasm in which it is situated by a well-defined membrane. Within the nucleus, during the process of reproduction, which we shall shortly describe, distinct bodies appear called chromosomes, which control the characteristics which a cell will pass on to its progeny; specific characteristics being regulated by separate parts of the chromosomes called *genes*. We shall have to say more about genetic inheritance shortly; the point to be made at present is that the function of the nucleus is to control the reproductive processes of the cell, and the characteristics which its progeny will inherit from it.

THE CYTOPLASM. Apart from the nucleus, the cytoplasm of a cell also contains a large number of microscopic granules, fat globules, and rod-shaped bodies called *mitochondria*. In general the function of the cytoplasm is the breakdown of food into energy and small molecules, and the synthesis of the structural materials of the cell. We shall discuss the biochemical reactions by which these processes take place in greater detail in the sections dealing with metabolism, but it should be noted here that while the cytoplasm has been called the factory of the cell, this distinction between the functions of the nucleus and cytoplasm cannot be made too rigidly.

Cell Reproduction

In general the growth of all living organisms occurs not by the growth of the cell itself, but by multiplication of the number of cells. This multiplication occurs as a result of the contents of the cell being doubled by replication followed by fission into two roughly equal parts, a process known as *mitosis* (see Figure 15). In the first stage of cellular reproduction the chromosomes (which in the resting stage are not individually identifiable) appear in the nucleus, each of which on inspection with a microscope can be seen to consist of two identical filaments called *chromatids*. As these chromosomes contract and thicken the membrane separating the nucleus from the cytoplasm disappears, and at the same time a spindle-like structure develops in the nucleus at the centre of which the chromosomes arrange themselves.

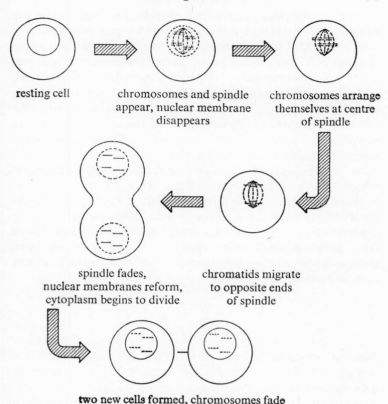

resting cell

chromosomes and spindle
appear, nuclear membrane
disappears

chromosomes arrange
themselves at centre
of spindle

spindle fades,
nuclear membranes reform,
cytoplasm begins to divide

chromatids migrate
to opposite ends
of spindle

two new cells formed, chromosomes fade

Fig. 15

During the next stage, the chromatids of each chromosome
separate and migrate to opposite ends of the spindle, thus forming
two identical sets. When this stage is complete the spindle disappears and two new nuclear membranes start to form, each
enclosing one set of chromatids.

In the final stage, the cytoplasm divides into approximately
equal halves, each of which contains a newly formed nucleus. The
two new cells thus created return to their resting state. The time
that elapses between fissions depends on a number of factors,

but the single-celled bacteria can double their numbers every half an hour in this way, if the conditions are propitious.

In Figure 15 it will be seen that we have illustrated a cell which contains only four chromosomes. In fact the number of chromosomes in a cell varies widely, depending upon the species to which it belongs. For example, human cells contain forty-six chromosomes, while those of the fruit fly (*Drosophila*) have only eight. The small number of chromosomes, and the comparatively large size of certain cells of the fruit fly, make it a favourite laboratory specimen for experiments in genetics.

As all single-celled organisms reproduce themselves in the manner which we have described, it is worth commenting that in a sense they can be said to be immortal (barring fatal accidents) – parts of them live for ever in the bodies of their progeny.

Having given, in the barest outline, the structure and method of reproduction of single-celled organisms, we may now investigate the way in which they have evolved into multicelled creatures, and, in particular, into man.

EVOLUTION

We shall return in the last chapter of this book to a summary of the current views concerning the origin of animate from inanimate matter. For the present purpose we must assume that some hundreds of millions of years ago there appeared (either in one place or in many places – it does not matter which) single-celled living organisms capable of regulating themselves and reproducing themselves in the manner which we have described. It may be that these primitive organisms were similar to the bacteria with which we are familiar, or it may be that they were a good deal more elementary even than these organisms. The essential, and generally accepted, hypothesis is that life as we have defined it originated with unicellular organisms, almost certainly in the sea.

Now we have said that living organisms are characterized by their ability to regulate and replicate themselves, processes which we are able, in general terms, to describe with reference to matter and energy. But there remains a third characteristic of living matter which we have not yet been able to explain in these material terms. This third characteristic is the *will to survive* – and in this sense survival implies not only the continued existence of the organism itself, but also its perpetuation by reproduction. Whether or not it will ever be possible to describe this characteristic of life in terms of chemistry and physics has long been a subject of debate. According to the mechanistic view, the will to survive, or the life-force, as it has been called, is no more than the sum of the physico-chemical properties of the component materials of the cell. On the other hand, there are those who believe that life has some metaphysical property which cannot be either expressed or interpreted in terms of the senses. Until a good deal more information is available concerning the biochemistry of the cell, this intriguing problem must remain unanswered; attempts at an answer in the present state of our knowledge must necessarily involve making assumptions which may well turn out in the future to have been unjustified.

In spite of our inability to understand it, the will to survive has, over the millions of years that life has inhabited the earth, been expressed in what is called *evolution*; that is the adaptation of living forms to their environment in such a way that they stand the best possible chance of perpetuating their species.

In the early stages of life on earth, the hazards presented by the environment were inanimate – broadly speaking the inclemency of the elements – but as life developed, or evolved, it became self-predatory so that the weaker and the smaller were consumed, or deprived of their food, by the stronger and the bigger. Thus only the best-adapted forms, that is the fittest organisms, were able to survive. These statements clearly imply that changes occur in the form of living matter in the course of its struggle to survive, and we must therefore now consider the mechanism of these changes. We have said earlier that inherited characteristics are controlled by the chromosomes which appear in the nucleus of a cell during mitosis, and that the individual inherited characteristics are controlled by the genes which form part of the chromosomes. It is therefore obvious that if genes remain unchanged for all time, there could be no evolution – that is no possibility of life-forms fundamentally changing their characteristics so as to be better adapted to their environment.

But in fact genes do *not* remain unchanged, they mutate (or alter) from time to time in a random manner, often as a result of exposure to ionizing radiations. In Chapter 10 we shall have something more to say about these radiations; for the present it must be accepted that there is a low level of background ionizing radiation from radioactive elements in the earth's crust and cosmic-ray reactions (see page 188, and page 190 for the effect of nuclear weapons). There are undoubtedly other undiscovered causes of genetic mutation, but the effect of ionizing radiations is confirmed by the fact that mutations can be brought about in the laboratory as a result of irradiation by such ionizing radiations as X-rays and γ-rays.

Now these random mutations which occur in nature will produce a wide variety of changes in the characteristics which an organism inherits, most of which will be to its disadvantage, but a few of which may be beneficial. Those characteristics which prove to be a disadvantage will either result in the death of the organism or will lead to a weak strain which will fare badly in competition with strains better adapted to cope with the vicissitudes of life. On the other hand, mutations which result in the inheritance of beneficial characteristics will give rise to strains that stand a better chance of survival than any other. This, then, is nature's way of selecting those forms of life which are best adapted for survival.

The whole history of evolution is a catalogue of this process, but we may take one example to illustrate the point. Imagine a primitive form of fish, which as a result of a genetic mutation, say some 300 million years ago, gave birth to an offspring whose fins were 'deformed' in such a way that it found that it was able to propel itself along the bottom of the sea-bed by 'walking' on its deformed fins. This fortunate fish would then be capable of exploring areas of very shallow water in which other fish would not dare to venture for fear of being stranded, and it would thereby gain an advantage in the relentless search for food. Consequently its progeny, which would also inherit this characteristic, would develop into a species specially selected by nature for survival. We may imagine just such a step as this in the evolution of amphibian from fish. Clearly a great deal of time, that is to say a great many generations, would be required to make any progress in the development of limbs as we know them, but, as it has taken some 500 million years for man to evolve from the first life-forms, this is in no way an obstacle to the theory of evolution.

But this is anticipating: we must return now to our primitive unicellular organism. It will be obvious that a single-celled organism reproducing by fission alone does not provide a great deal of scope for the sort of competitive evolution we have been discussing. In fact, it can be observed in the laboratory that after many successive generations of reproduction by fission, in the absence of any spectacular mutations, cells often develop a degree of laziness that can be expressed as the loss of the will to survive.

At some stage, then, in the development of unicellular organisms, a new stimulus was required to augment the effect of genetic mutation. This stimulus was provided by an amended form of reproduction – reproduction by the fusion of two cells instead of the fission of one. This was the first step towards sexual reproduction, and it was undoubtedly taken when evolution had only reached the stage of the more complex unicellular organisms.

The benefit of this form of reproduction is achieved as a result of the contents of two nuclei being pooled in such a way that a new cell is formed which inherits half its chromosomes from each of its parent cells. This cell then reproduces by fission in the normal way, but is invigorated by the admixture of the contents of the two genetic reservoirs. The cells capable of fusion in this way are called *gametes*, and the fertilized cell, produced as a result of the fusion of the two gamete nuclei, each of which has half the normal number of chromosomes, is called a *zygote*.

With the development of reproduction by fusion the stage was set for the next step towards greater complexity and greater adaptation of species – the multicellular organism. But this step was almost certainly taken by way of the half-measure of a cell colony. Once a group of cells had, by living together in a colony, enhanced their survival value, it could only have been a matter of time before some of the cells in the colony developed specialized functions; thus certain cells would perform particular tasks necessary to the survival of the colony while other cells would perform quite different functions. Clearly the first and most important specialized function would be that of reproducing another set of cells aware of the advantages of colonial life. Reproduction of the whole assembly of cells would then become the specific task of one particular cell whose genetic material would contain the information that living in a colony was a beneficial practice.

Fission would not be a suitable way for such a highly specialized cell to reproduce, whereas the fusion of one such cell with another from a different colony, or a different part of the same colony, would have the advantage of sharing the 'secrets of survival' that each had learnt. In time these cells specific to the function of reproduction evolved into the female eggs and the male sperms which characterize sexual reproduction in the higher life-forms. Of course, as cell colonies developed into multicellular organisms, the reproductive cells would not be the only ones to specialize their function: every cell in the organism would develop in such a way that it became specialized, or *differentiated* as the correct term is, so that it could only perform one function. Groups of these differentiated cells within the organism would then combine to form the tissues and organs of the highly developed creatures with which the earth now abounds.

This is not the place to set out the details of the process of evolution, but in Figure 16 we give a very incomplete and schematic diagram illustrating its general trend. The time-scale is, of course, extremely approximate – such figures are obtained from a geological assessment of fossils and cannot therefore be expected to be accurate.

In this diagram we have used an abridged form of the internationally agreed system of classification, in which life-forms are successively divided into *kingdoms, sub-kingdoms, phyla, classes, orders, families, genera,* and finally *species.*

It will be seen from the diagram that very early in the history of life, while it was still in the unicellular form, it divided into the two kingdoms of animals and plants. The essential difference between these kingdoms is that while most plants are able to make the organic molecules which they require by photosynthesis

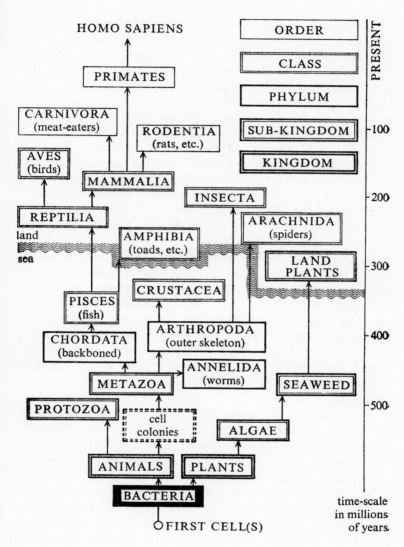

Fig. 16

(see page 105), animals are without this ability and therefore depend for their food either on plants or on other animals.

Animals are next divided into the sub-kingdoms of *Protozoa* (single-celled organisms) and *Metazoa* (multicelled organisms). The Metazoa evolved into eleven different phyla, not all of which are shown in the diagram, but it will be seen that the phylum of *Chordata* (animals with backbones) evolved into the classes *Pisces* (fish), *Amphibia* (frogs, toads, etc.), *Reptilia* (snakes, lizards, etc.), and *Aves* (birds). At the stage of amphibians and reptiles, life finally emerged from the sea and invaded the land which by this time was fairly liberally covered with the land-plants. This invasion of the land led to the evolution of the class of *Mammalia* which contains all the animals with warm blood and hair which suckle their young. Of the various orders of mammals the most highly developed are, of course, the *primates* (man, apes, etc.) from which during only the last million or so years the species of *Homo sapiens* has evolved.

We must conclude this extremely brief account of evolution by saying that not all of nature's experiments in adaptation have been successful; many creatures (dinosaurs for example) developed in such a cumbersome way that they were unequal to the challenge presented to them by cataclysmic changes in environment, and they therefore became extinct. On the other hand, some of nature's most elementary Protozoa (such as amoeba) and bacteria have been so successful in their limited way that they have continued to survive throughout nearly the whole course of evolution.

With regard to the future trend of evolution, and the vexed question of whether or not man is the ultimate product of nature, not very much need be said. This is largely a matter for speculation, although at this late stage of the evolutionary process genetic mutations are almost always deleterious. However, it should be added that, since the advent of man, evolution has acquired a new component. The secrets of survival are no longer confined to purely genetic mechanisms of transmission from generation to generation. With the dominance of mind, the development of speech, and the growth of social culture, man is able to pass on to his progeny verbal and written information concerning techniques of survival. Furthermore, the relentless operation of natural selection is greatly restricted in a civilized society in which the strong care for the weak and both have equal opportunities for reproduction. Such considerations, however, belong to the study of social eugenics and are not within our present scope.

BIOCHEMICAL REACTIONS

Having outlined the great diversity of forms which life has adopted during some 500 million to 3,000 million years of evolution, we may now concentrate our attention on the biochemical reactions upon which living processes depend.

Fortunately, although there are some one-and-a-half million different species of plants and animals we shall find that much the same fundamental processes are common to all of them. For example, all green plants depend for their basic materials on the process of photosynthesis which is controlled by the compound *chlorophyll* (see page 105), while all animals with blood circulation rely on the transport of oxygen throughout their bodies by the related compound *haemoglobin*. There are also many examples of reactions which are identical in both plants and animals. For instance yeast, which is classified as a plant, is able to bring about the conversion of glucose into ethyl alcohol (as in brewing) by a series of reactions, one stage of which involves the formation of pyruvic acid. The reaction from glucose to pyruvic acid takes place in eight stages, and the same series of reactions, in the same eight stages, takes place in the muscle-cells of man. This is extremely strong evidence that yeast and man have a common ancestry, a fact which would be expected from inspection of Figure 16. We must now look more closely at the sort of reactions which take place within cells.

Metabolism

In general, the purposes of the biochemical reactions, which take place within a cell during its resting stage, are the conversion of food into suitable materials for the construction of the cell components and the provision of energy to sustain its functions. These reactions collectively constitute what is known as the cell's *metabolism*. Now metabolism can be divided into two types: one being the breaking down of food into simple molecules and free energy (*katabolism*), and the other the synthesis, from these and other molecules, of the complex molecules required for the cell's construction or energy conservation (*anabolism*).

Thus if A represents a cell-food, and F a complex molecule required by the cell, the generalized process of metabolism may be represented by the sequence of reactions:

$$A \rightarrow B \rightarrow C \rightarrow D \rightarrow E \rightarrow F$$

Of course, the number of stages will depend on the materials concerned, but in general some of them will be katabolic and some will be anabolic.

Enzymes

Biochemical reactions are extremely dependent upon catalysts (see page 68), or *enzymes* as they are called in biochemistry; each stage of a series of reactions requiring its own specific enzyme. Every cell contains a great number of enzymes, and their study is of paramount importance in biochemistry.

While most enzymes cannot make a reaction occur that would not take place in their absence, they speed up reactions so that they can occur at the temperatures and other conditions which prevail within living organisms. Like inorganic catalysts, enzymes are not consumed during reactions, although they may form loose complexes with the molecules (called the *substrate*) they provoke into reaction.

The catalytic effect of an enzyme depends on the shape and size of its molecule and the number and position of its 'active centres', for it is only when these active centres come into contact with the substrate molecule that catalysis occurs. For this reason the action of an enzyme can be easily inhibited by the combination of one of these active centres with some other atom or molecule. For example, the poisonous nature of such metals as arsenic and mercury is due to their inhibition of enzymes vital to the life of cells. It should be noted, however, that not all metals are poisonous to enzymes; indeed the presence of some metals is essential to the proper function of certain enzymes.

Another way in which the action of an enzyme can be upset

is called *competitive inhibition*; this happens when the active centre of an enzyme attaches itself to a substrate which is similar to, but not identical with, the correct one. The action of sulphonamide drugs is believed to occur as a result of competitive inhibition in the following way. For their growth many bacteria need the compound amino-benzoic acid, and as traces of this compound are found in the blood of animals, these bacteria live a parasitic life in animal blood. When sulphonamide drugs are administered, the compound sulphanilamide is liberated in the blood stream, which is very similar in shape to amino-benzoic acid:

$$NH_2 \!-\!\!\bigcirc\!\!-\! COOH \qquad NH_2 \!-\!\!\bigcirc\!\!-\! SO_2NH_2$$

amino-benzoic acid   sulphanilamide

The bacterial enzymes then form a complex with the sulphanilamide molecules as substrate. The bacteria are therefore starved of amino-benzoic acid, and die, or cease to multiply, which is, of course, the purpose of the drug.

Enzymes, the names of most of which end in the letters 'ase', all belong to a most important group of complex nitrogenous organic compounds called *proteins*. Although all enzymes are proteins, not all proteins are enzymes, and, as we shall see, other proteins are of vital importance in the chemistry of living matter. We must therefore say something about this important group of compounds, and return later to a discussion of enzymes and their connexion with inheritance.

Proteins

All proteins are formed from combinations of units called *amino acids* with the general formula:

$$\begin{array}{c} R \\ | \\ CH\!-\!\!-\!COOH \\ | \\ NH_2 \end{array}$$

The 'R' group may take many different forms; in the simplest amino acid of all, glycine, it consists of one hydrogen atom. If

two amino acids join together with the elimination of a molecule
of water, a peptide linkage is formed:

$$\begin{array}{c} R_1 \\ | \\ CH-CO\boxed{OH + H}NH-CH \\ / \qquad\qquad\qquad | \\ NH_2 \qquad\qquad\quad R_2 \end{array} \quad \overset{COOH}{\underset{}{}} \longrightarrow \begin{array}{c} R_1 \\ | \\ CH \quad NH \quad COOH \\ / \quad \backslash \quad / \\ NH_2 \quad CO \quad CH \\ \qquad\qquad | \\ \qquad\qquad R_2 \end{array}$$

This compound is called a *dipeptide*, while three amino acids
linked together yield a *tripeptide*. The addition of more than three
amino acids makes a polypeptide chain:

$$\begin{array}{c} R_1 \qquad\qquad\qquad\qquad R_3 \\ | \qquad\qquad\qquad\qquad | \\ CH \quad NH \quad CO \quad CH \quad NH \quad CO \\ / \quad \backslash \quad / \quad \backslash \quad / \quad \backslash \quad / \quad \backslash \\ NH \quad CO \quad CH \quad NH \quad CO \quad CH \\ \qquad\qquad | \qquad\qquad\qquad\qquad | \\ \qquad\qquad R_2 \qquad\qquad\qquad\qquad R_4 \end{array}$$

It is not necessary for the 'R' groups to be all different from
each other; in some chains consisting of several hundreds of
amino acids the same groups may appear at regular intervals.
There are, in fact, some twenty to twenty-five different amino
acids of biochemical importance represented by these various
'R' groups.

Proteins are formed when these polypeptide chains link
together, thus:

The 'R' groups incorporated in the polypeptide chains and the type of linkages between them will determine the nature of the particular protein. Some proteins are long and thin, such as hair, wool, and silk; while some are short and fat, such as the enzymes which we have been discussing.

Proteins are obviously very complicated substances, and in most cases their precise structures have not been worked out, but in 1954 the complete structure of the hormone insulin was identified.

The specificity of enzymes is related to their structure, and resides within the individual 'R' groups contained by the molecule.

THE ENERGY OF BIOCHEMICAL REACTIONS

We have said that during cell metabolism food is converted into cell components or is broken down to yield its stored chemical energy. As metabolism proceeds in stages, it is to be expected that during some of these stages energy will be liberated, while in other stages it will remain stored in the reacting molecules.

Thus, in the generalized example (page 100) of the conversion of the food 'A' into the cell component 'F', energy may be liberated, say, in the stages B → C and D → F. This energy, having been detached from the metabolic sequence A . . . F, is then either used to energize some cell function (such as motion or temperature control) or it is re-stored on a longer-term basis in a special type of molecule which we shall call Ⓟ, for use on some later occasion. These events are illustrated diagrammatically in Figure 17.

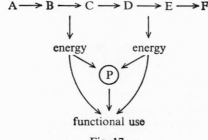

Fig. 17

The chemical energy of a molecule is stored in the bonds which hold the atoms together, so that when a reaction takes place these bonds will be rearranged, and consequently there will be an energy-change in the system (see page 131). Some bonds may be regarded in this way as being 'energy-rich', that is to say they are bonds which will give off more energy than others when they are broken, and these bonds are of special importance in biochemical reactions.

By far the commonest and most significant of the energy-rich bonds are those formed between phosphorus and certain organic compounds, and of these organic phosphates the most important is the compound adenosine triphosphate, generally known as ATP. Adenosine is a compound formed from the nitrogenous base adenine and the sugar ribose (see page 106); ATP, therefore, which has two energy-rich bonds, has the structure:

ribose

When ATP loses one of its energy-rich phosphate bonds it becomes the diphosphate ADP – also an important compound which we shall meet again.

Compounds which are formed from a *base*, a *sugar*, and a *phosphate* are called *nucleotides* and, as we shall see later, these compounds are of great significance not only in metabolic processes, but also in genetic inheritance. It may be said, therefore, that if there is a 'secret' of life it lies on the molecular level within the nucleotides.

Cell Foods

Having given a brief description of how energy is stored during biochemical processes we may now consider the metabolic reactions which we have illustrated by the general series A → F (page 100).

These considerations must clearly start by looking at the foods which are required by cells. There are, in fact, three types of organic compound required by cells for their sustenance: *carbohydrates*, *fats*, and *proteins*. Proteins we have already mentioned, carbohydrates and fats we shall discuss shortly, but before doing so we must say a few words about photosynthesis, for it is upon this process that plants, and therefore animals, depend for the manufacture of these basic foods.

Photosynthesis

Plants, as we have already mentioned, are able to manufacture their own foods from water, carbon dioxide in the atmosphere, and the inorganic salts (phosphates, nitrates, etc.) which they extract from the earth. This process, which is energized by light from the sun, is called *photosynthesis*. Animals lack this ability completely, and are therefore entirely dependent on plants, or on other animals in the case of Carnivores (meat-eaters), for their basic foods.

Although the process of photosynthesis is essential for the continuation of all life on earth, we are still a long way from completely understanding it. We do know, however, that when sunlight falls on green plants it is absorbed within their cells by small particles called *chloroplasts*; these particles contain various molecules the most important of which are the *chlorophylls*, a group of green pigments to which plants largely owe their green colour. In some way, which is not yet understood, chlorophyll is able to turn the energy of sunlight into chemical energy which is stored in ATP molecules. These energy-rich molecules are then able, through a complex series of reactions each of which requires a specific enzyme, to activate the conversion of carbon dioxide and water into a form of sugar, glucose. The reaction can be written:

$$6CO_2 + 6H_2O \rightarrow C_6H_{12}O_6 + 6O_2$$
$$(glucose)$$

although written in this form the equation conceals the intricacy of the many stages it encompasses.

Plants are not only able to make their own sugar, they can also convert this sugar into starch and cellulose (all carbohydrates) as well as fats and proteins. In order to understand the biochemical reactions involved, it will now be necessary to say something about carbohydrates and fats.

Carbohydrates

We have said that carbohydrates include sugars, starches, and cellulose – all these substances, as their collective name suggests, are water compounds (hydrates) of carbon. They all have the general formula $C_n(H_2O)_m$ where the letters n and m determine the type of carbohydrate in question.

Carbohydrates are usually classified as follows:

1. Monosaccharides – which are sugars.
2. Disaccharides – also sugars.
3. Polysaccharides – which are starches and cellulose.

Each of these groups will now be discussed separately.

MONOSACCHARIDES. These sugar compounds can be again divided into two classes: *pentoses*, with five carbon atoms, and *hexoses*, with six carbon atoms. Of the pentoses, only the sugar ribose is important, occurring, as we have seen, in ATP and ADP, as well as in the nucleic acids which we shall discuss on page 121. Ribose has the formula $C_5H_{10}O_5$, and the structure:

which may also be written:

The hexoses are typified by the sugar glucose, which occurs in grapes and other plants, as well as in the blood of animals; biochemically it is by far the most important sugar. Its structure is similar to that of ribose except that it has an extra —CHOH group; its formula is therefore $C_6H_{12}O_6$, and its structure may be drawn:

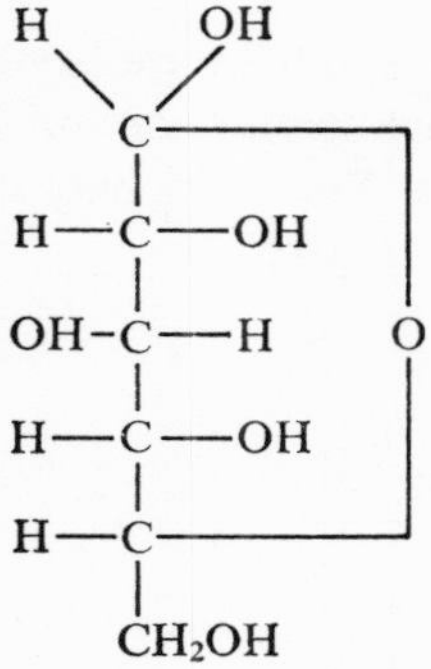

or more commonly:

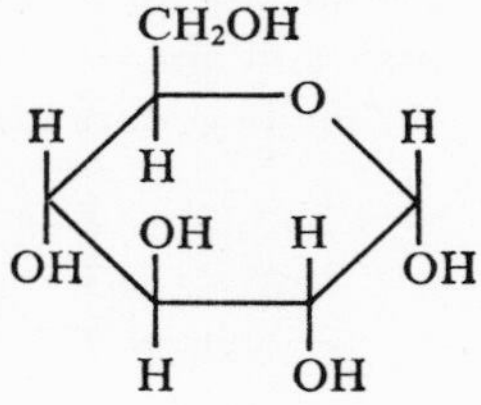

DISACCHARIDES. These compounds, as their name implies, are made from two Monosaccharides from which a molecule of water has been eliminated, and they have the general formula $C_{12}H_{22}O_{11}$. Biochemically the most important sugar in this group is sucrose, which occurs in cane and beet sugar; the sugar which we buy at the grocers is very largely this type. It has the structure:

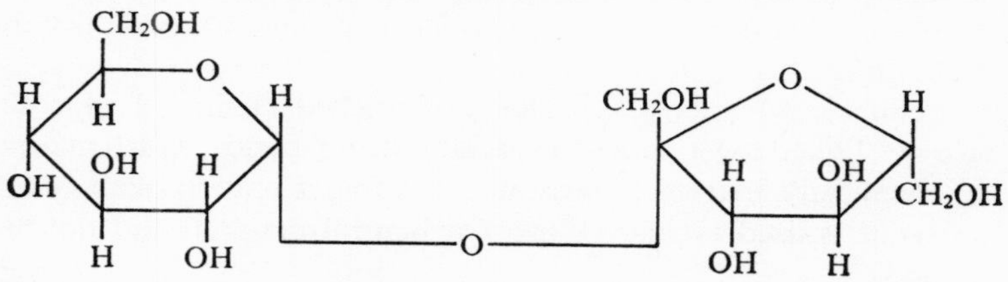

Other disaccharides of importance are *maltose*, which consists of two glucose molecules, and *lactose*, which is found in the milk of mammals.

POLYSACCHARIDES. Polysaccharides consist of chains of monosaccharides linked together, and they therefore have the general formula $(C_6H_{10}O_5)_n$. They can be classified into *starches* and *cellulose*, about each of which we must now say a few words.

Starches occur in two main forms. The first, *amylose*, consists of a straight chain of some 200 to 500 glucose molecules:

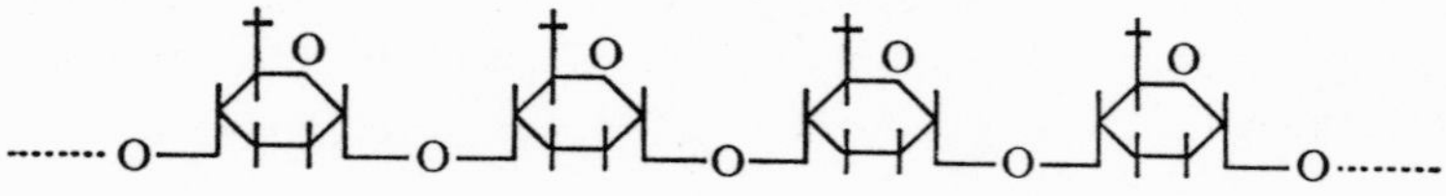

The second form, *amylopectin*, is a branched-chain molecule containing up to 1,000 glucose molecules, each branch of which may contain twenty to thirty glucose groups. The branching of the chain occurs in this way:

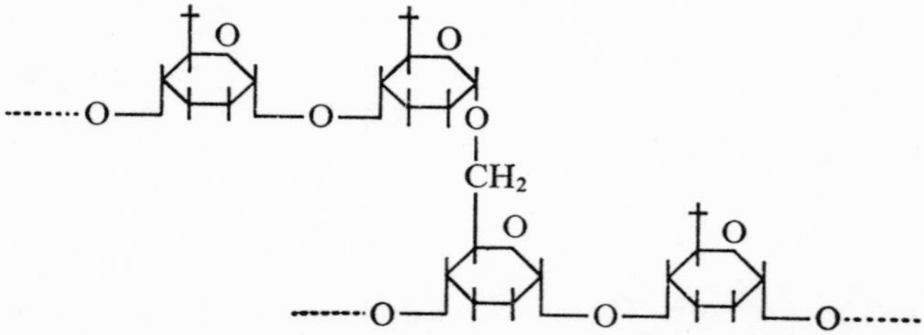

Potato starch contains about 20 per cent amylose and 80 per cent amylopectin, but other plants have different proportions of the two starches. In general, plants store starch in their tubers and seeds, where it acts as a food reservoir from which monosaccharides can be liberated when required. Animal cells store starch in the form of *glycogen* which is similar to amylopectin but is more highly branched.

Cellulose consists of parallel unbranched chains of glucose groups, linked together with especially strong bonds, which makes it, chemically, extremely resistant. It is found only in plant cells, where it is used exclusively as a structural material and not as a food.

As it is chemically very resistant, cellulose can only be broken down in nature in the presence of special enzymes called *cellulases*, which are produced by certain bacteria. *Herbivores* (grass-eating animals such as the horse and the cow) have colonies of such bacteria in their alimentary tract, and are therefore able to digest the cellulose of grass, making use of the sugars into which these enzymes break it down. This mutually beneficial relationship between herbivores and bacteria is called *symbiosis*.

With this brief outline of the chemistry of carbohydrates in mind we are now able to proceed to an examination of their metabolism in living organisms.

Carbohydrate Metabolism

Of the carbohydrates only sugar molecules are sufficiently small to pass through cell walls; starch and cellulose molecules are too large and therefore have to be broken down outside the cell. For this purpose some cells are capable of secreting enzymes which catalyse the breakdown of polysaccharides outside the cell. Saliva and pancreatic secretions contain such enzymes and, as we have seen, certain bacteria produce enzymes which catalyse the breakdown of cellulose. In order to enter the cell, then, carbohydrates have to be broken down into sugars, and as by far the most important sugar in this respect is glucose we shall examine the metabolism of this molecule within the cell.

The oxidation of glucose into carbon dioxide, water, and energy can be represented by the following equation, which it will be noted is exactly the reverse of photosynthesis:

$$C_6H_{12}O_6 + 6O_2 \rightarrow 6CO_2 + 6H_2O + \text{energy}$$

As we shall see in Chapter 8, combustion consists very largely of the oxidation of carbon to carbon dioxide and the oxidation of hydrogen to water with the release of energy; clearly therefore, this glucose reaction is a combustion reaction. However, in living matter reactions take place in stages during the course of which energy is temporarily stored in such energy-rich molecules as ATP. Furthermore, many biochemical reactions are reversible and the direction which they take will depend on the circumstances and the requirements of the cell. Therefore, while it is true to say that carbohydrate metabolism consists of the combustion of glucose, this statement is a somewhat misleading over-simplification.

Chemically, glucose is a relatively inert molecule, and it is therefore one of the many functions of ATP to convert it into an active compound; this it does by giving it one of its phosphate bonds, changing in the process from ATP to ADP. The formation of glucose phosphate in this way is catalysed by the enzyme *hexokinase*:

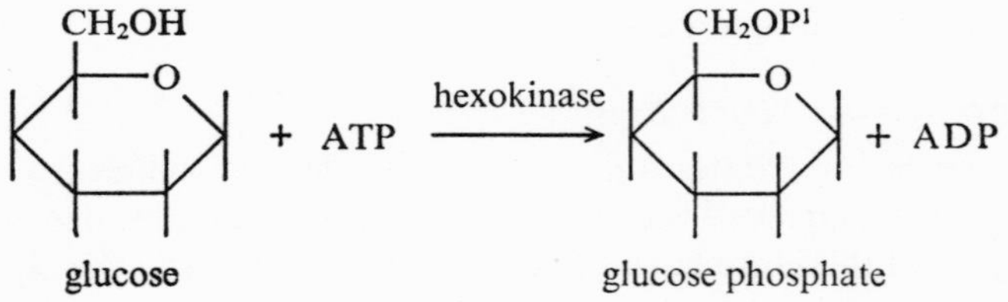

$$\underset{\text{glucose}}{\text{CH}_2\text{OH} \quad \bigcirc} \quad + \text{ ATP} \quad \xrightarrow{\text{hexokinase}} \quad \underset{\text{glucose phosphate}}{\text{CH}_2\text{OP}^1 \quad \bigcirc} \quad + \text{ ADP}$$

Although glucose can diffuse through a cell wall, glucose phosphate cannot do so, and thus, in a sense, ATP can be said to draw glucose into the cell, as well as activating it for further reaction.

Once this reactive glucose phosphate has been formed within the cell, one of two things may happen to it: either it can be built up into a polysaccharide to act as a food reservoir for the future (and the manufacture of cellulose in the case of plants), or it can be broken down further with the subsequent liberation of energy.

Looking first at the build-up to polysaccharides, it has been shown that the conversion of glucose phosphate into starch takes place in two reversible stages. In plant cells the enzymes present direct the reaction so that amylose and amylopectin are formed, while in animal cells slightly different enzymes produce glycogen. Animal cells store this water-insoluble glycogen, so that if their supply of glucose is cut off for any reason, they have a reservoir of food in the form of starch. Thus, in the absence of glucose, the glucose phosphate-starch reaction goes into reverse, so that starch is broken down into glucose phosphate.

Bearing in mind the manufacture of glucose from carbon dioxide during photosynthesis, the metabolic processes may be represented as in Figure 18a.

We now have to consider how glucose phosphate is broken down with the evolution of energy. In both plant and animal cells this process can take place in one of two ways, that is either in the presence of oxygen (called an *aerobic process*) or partly in the absence of oxygen (called an *anaerobic process*).

In the aerobic process, glucose phosphate is broken down,

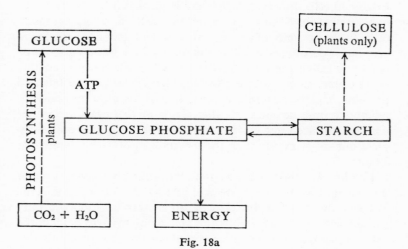

Fig. 18a

with the further assistance of ATP and various enzymes, in a series of complex reactions which we need not describe, into carbon dioxide and energy. In the anaerobic process, with the help of ADP, after seven stages the compound pyruvic acid ($CH_3CO.COOH$) is formed:

$$\text{Glucose-Phosphate} + 2ADP \rightarrow 2 \text{ Pyruvic Acid} + 2ATP$$

In this way, it will be seen that the breakdown of glucose in the absence of oxygen yields pyruvic acid and two energy-rich ATP molecules – a process called *anaerobic glycolysis*. This process is most important to animals in circumstances in which they need more oxygen than their blood can supply (e.g., a sudden energy requirement such as a jump), for anaerobic glycolysis can provide energy in the form of ATP.

We have already mentioned that the pathway from glucose to pyruvic acid is exactly the same in animal cells as it is in fermentation by yeast. However, yeast contains two additional enzymes, not present in animal cells, which convert the pyruvic acid first into acetaldehyde and then into ethyl alcohol, thus:

$$CH_3CO \cdot COOH \rightarrow CO_2 + CH_3CHO \xrightarrow{H_2} CH_3CH_2OH + CO_2$$
$$\text{Pyruvic acid} \qquad\qquad \text{Acetaldehyde} \quad \text{Ethyl alcohol}$$

In animal cells, however, lactic acid is formed from pyruvic acid in anaerobic conditions – an important reaction in animal muscle cells. In the presence of oxygen, pyruvic acid does not form lactic acid but is decomposed within the cell by a complicated series of reactions called the *citric-acid cycle*. As we shall see later, this series of reactions is also used in the final breakdown of fats and proteins, and is therefore a most important clearing-house of metabolic intermediates. As the details of this cycle are rather complex we need not go into them here, but we may now complete our diagram outlining the metabolism of carbohydrates in Figure 18b.

Finally, we must mention that the anaerobic conversion of glucose phosphate to pyruvic acid is reversible provided that the appropriate enzymes are present, so in this way glucose (and starch) can be made within the cell from pyruvic acid if the external source of glucose is reduced. In the case of plants this

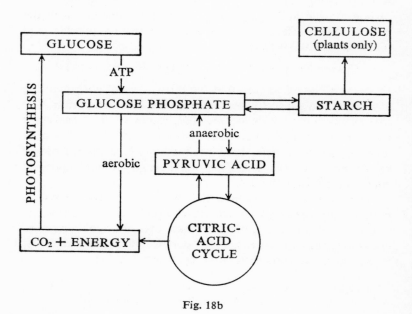

Fig. 18b

reaction is not important, of course, because they can make their own glucose by photosynthesis, and seeds can draw on their reservoir of starch.

After this brief survey of carbohydrate metabolism, we may now pass to the fats and their metabolism.

The Lipids

We have said that one of the three basic foods required by living organisms is fats. Fats, however, form part of a larger group of organic compounds known as *lipids*, which may be classified as:

1. Simple lipids – fats and waxes.
2. Compound lipids – phospholipids and glycolipids.
3. Steroids.

SIMPLE LIPIDS. Fats are simple lipids formed by the combination of glycerol and fatty acids. Glycerol, it will be remembered, has the structure (see page 75):

$$CH_2OH$$
$$|$$
$$CH.OH$$
$$|$$
$$CH_2OH$$

and fats, therefore, have the general formula:

$$CH_2OOC.R_1$$
$$|$$
$$CHOOC.R_2$$
$$|$$
$$CH_2OOC.R_3$$

Natural fats are mixtures of such compounds in which the 'R' groups represent fatty acids with from four to thirty carbon atoms, but by far the commonest are esters of palmitic acid:

$$C_{15}H_{31}.COOH$$

stearic acid

$$C_{17}H_{35}.COOH$$

and oleic acid

$$C_{17}H_{33}.COOH$$

Nearly all the fatty acids which occur in nature have even numbers of carbon atoms and, of the three acids mentioned above, only one, oleic acid, is unsaturated (i.e., contains a double bond, see page 73). In general the more unsaturated acid a fat contains, the lower is its melting-point – for example olive oil is nearly all oleic acid and is therefore a liquid at normal temperatures. (An oil is simply a liquid fat, and waxes, which do not concern us here, are combinations of fatty acids with alcohols other than glycerol.)

COMPOUND LIPIDS. The Phospholipids are compounds made from glycerol, fatty acids, a phosphate, and a nitrogenous base:

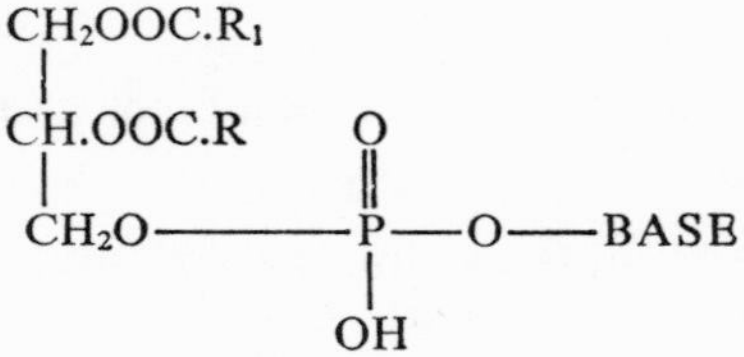

$$
\begin{array}{l}
CH_2OOC.R_1 \\
| \\
CH.OOC.R \qquad O \\
| \qquad\qquad\quad \| \\
CH_2O\!-\!\!-\!\!-\!\!-\!\!-\!\!-P\!-\!O\!-\!\!-BASE \\
\qquad\qquad\quad | \\
\qquad\qquad\quad OH
\end{array}
$$

These compounds are required by cells in the construction of their membranes; they also occur in blood plasma and in the yolk of eggs. The glycolipids are also very complex substances, but not very much is known about their function in living organisms.

STEROIDS. These compounds are involved in a variety of processes, such as the calcification of teeth and bone, the distribution of hair, etc., but many of their activities are not properly understood. A typical example of this group is *cholesterol*, which occurs in animals; its excessive production in man has been suspected of being a contributory cause of coronary thrombosis.

These remarkable compounds are all based on the following structure, to which a variety of side groups can be attached:

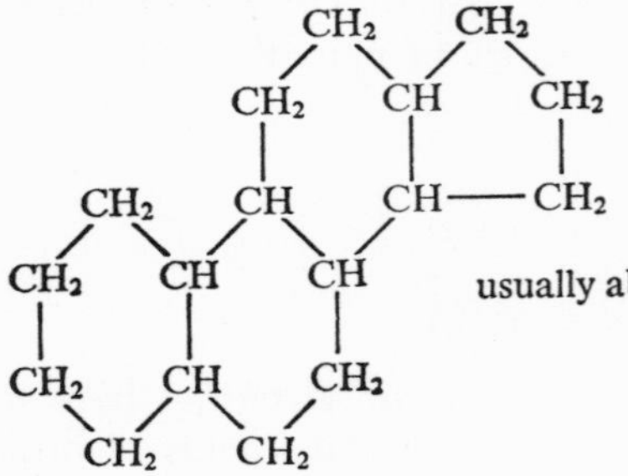

$$
\begin{array}{c}
CH_2 \quad CH_2 \\
CH_2 \quad CH \quad CH_2 \\
CH_2 \quad CH \quad CH\!-\!CH_2 \\
CH_2 \quad CH \quad CH \\
CH_2 \quad CH \quad CH_2 \\
CH_2 \quad CH_2
\end{array}
$$

usually abbreviated to:

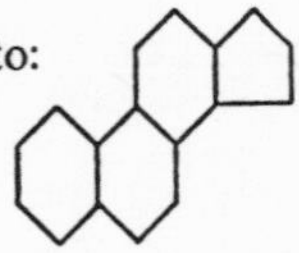

Lipid Metabolism

Fat is the most compact form in which food is stored in the body, and it is worth noting that its complete oxidation yields twice as much water as can be obtained from either carbohydrate or protein. The breakdown of fats by cells starts by hydrolysis into glycerol and fatty acids in the presence of enzymes called *lipases*:

$$
\begin{array}{lll}
CH_2OOC.R & & CH_2OH \\
| & \xrightleftharpoons{\text{LIPASES}} & | \\
CH.OOC.R \quad + \quad 3H_2O & & CH.OH \quad + \quad 3R.COOH \\
| & & | \\
CH_2OOC.R & & CH_2OH \\
\end{array}
$$

glycerol   fatty acid

This is a reversible reaction, the direction of which will depend on conditions in the cell.

The glycerol so formed is converted into glucose, with the help of ATP, via the intermediate stage of glycero-phosphate. The fatty acids, again with the help of ATP, are broken down through a variety of stages, the last of which form part of the citric-acid cycle, into carbon dioxide and energy.

In Figure 18c the metabolism of fats is added to our diagram illustrating the metabolism of carbohydrates.

The breakdown of fatty acids through the citric-acid cycle can be made reversible in certain circumstances, although the reverse reactions proceed by slightly different steps which are not shown in the diagram. It will be seen, therefore, that fats and carbo-hydrates are interconvertible within cells, but for reasons which are not yet clear most cells prefer carbohydrates to any other type of food. To complete our brief survey of cell metabolism we must now look at the way in which proteins are broken down.

Protein Metabolism

We have already outlined the general structure of proteins (see page 101), and seen that they consist of very large molecules; they cannot therefore be expected to diffuse through cell walls and have to be broken down outside the cell into their constituent amino acids. This process is catalysed by enzymes called *proteinases* and *peptidases*. For example, in man the stomach

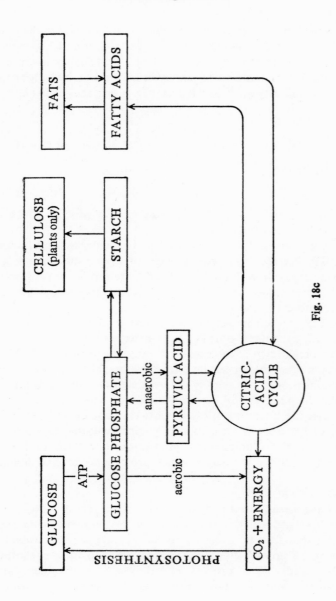

Fig. 18c

contains a typical peptidase called *pepsin* and the duodenum another called *trypsin*, which break down proteins into their amino acids, just as polysaccharides are broken down into their constituent monosaccharides.

Such enzymes as these are, of course, secreted by specialized cells in the body, but similar enzymes also occur within cells because cellular proteins are continuously being synthesized and broken down as part of the normal process of cell metabolism. One of two things, therefore, may happen to an amino acid which enters a cell: either it will be decomposed or it will be used in the synthesis of some other protein.

Looking first at the breakdown of amino acids, and without going into detail, we may say that they are either broken down into pyruvic acid or into one of the constituents of the citric-acid cycle. With some amino acids, ammonia is formed; as this is toxic to most cells, it is converted into urea by a series of reactions which may be summed up thus:

$$CO_2 + 2NH_3 \longrightarrow CO{\overset{\displaystyle NH_2}{\underset{\displaystyle NH_2}{\big\langle}}} + H_2O$$

$$\text{ammonia} \qquad\qquad \text{urea}$$

In the higher animals, of course, urea is disposed of by the body in the urine.

As regards the synthesis of particular amino acids in the cell, different forms of life have different requirements. For example, there are eight amino acids which man cannot make for himself in his body-cells, and these so-called 'essential amino acids' have to be supplied in his food. Other amino acids, however, can be synthesized by various processes, which use pyruvic acid, or one of the constituents of the citric-acid cycle, as a starting-point.

The order in which these amino acids join together in the cell to form proteins is still something of a mystery, but we shall return to this point later. In the meantime we may add protein metabolism to complete our general metabolic diagram (see Figure 18d).

This diagram which we have built up is, of course, a gross over-simplification of the great number of reactions which do, or can, take place within cells, but it shows the general outline of such processes and the way in which the citric-acid cycle acts as a clearing-house of intermediates for the interconversion of carbohydrates, fats, and proteins.

Finally, on the subject of metabolism, it should be said that many of the enzymes of the citric-acid cycle, as well as those which attack fatty acids, are contained in the mitochondria whose presence in the cytoplasm of cells we noted on page 90.

Metabolic Control

The very sketchy outline we have given of cell metabolism does not tell us how a man, or even an amoeba, works, for we have not said anything about the way in which these metabolic processes are controlled. Indeed, this is a subject about which not very much is known, particularly in multicellular organisms.

In single-celled organisms it appears that control results from a 'feedback' principle depending on the relative concentrations of the various foods and intermediates which exist in the cell. If, for instance, the concentration of glucose falls, this information is fed back to the starch reservoir which breaks down to the extent required to bring the concentration of glucose back to normal. Similarly, if oxygen is in short supply, and energy cannot be obtained by oxidation, molecules such as ATP liberate their stored energy. The citric-acid cycle appears to play an important part in these mechanisms, being very sensitive to the concentration of each of its constituents.

In multicellular organisms, and in the higher animals in particular, this question of the control of metabolism is, of course, very much more complex and elaborate. Co-ordination of body functions is brought about by a group of 'chemical messengers' called *hormones*, which are produced by special glands and which circulate in the blood-stream. These hormones are either proteins, steroids, or in some cases quite simple molecules. However, the biochemistry of their functions is not fully understood and is a subject of contemporary research.

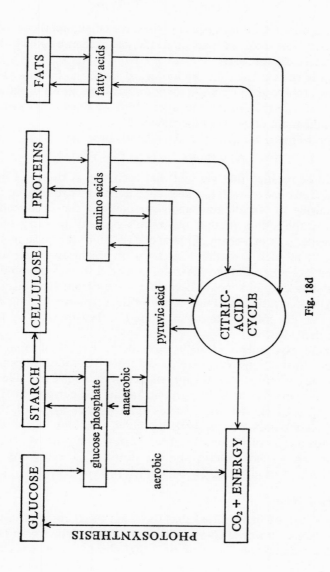

Fig. 18d

GENETIC INHERITANCE

Having outlined the processes by which cells maintain themselves we must now look, once again, at the mechanism by which they reproduce themselves.

We have said that, on the biological level, the factors which control reproduction are the chromosomes and genes in the cell nuclei; it is therefore these entities which we must now examine from the point of view of biochemistry.

Returning to our generalized metabolic process:

$$A \rightarrow B \rightarrow C \rightarrow D \rightarrow E \rightarrow F$$

it will be recalled that we said that each step is catalysed by a specific enzyme. Now it has been shown that, by exposing certain organisms to X-radiation, genetic mutations can occur which destroy the ability of that organism's progeny to carry out a particular step in a chain of metabolic reactions. For example, as a result of such a mutation a strain of organisms might arise which lacks the ability to make compound E from compound D. This state of affairs would become apparent from the unusually high concentration of D in the cells of the organism, and the fact that they are only able to manufacture F if they are supplied with E in their diet.

These experiments clearly point to the hypothesis that the genetic instructions which are passed from generation to generation are concerned with the inheritance of an ability to make the right enzyme for the right purpose. In fact the current theory is that for each enzyme which occurs in, or is made by, a cell, there is a corresponding gene. Thus the child who inherits from his parents a mop of red hair has been born with a gene which produces an enzyme whose specific function is catalysing the synthesis of a red dye in the cells which produce hair.

Nucleic Acids

While it must be admitted that the exact mechanism of genetic inheritance by way of enzymes has not yet been fully worked out, it has been known for some time that chromosomes consist of thread-like molecules of a substance called *deoxyribonucleic acid* (DNA for short), which has the structure:

As we saw when discussing ATP, compounds made up from a base, a sugar, and a phosphate are called nucleotides, and therefore DNA molecules are *polynucleotides*, differing from each other in the types of bases which they incorporate. The sugar is in all cases a derivative of ribose called deoxyribose; but there are four different types of bases which occur in these chains, and it is the order of the arrangement of these bases which constitutes some sort of code on the basis of which specific enzyme proteins are synthesized.

It has further been ascertained that chromosomes actually consist of two identical polynucleotide chains linked together by special bonds between the bases. These two chains are wound together into a helical spring-shaped structure, and the tightness of the winding of the spring is one of the factors controlling which bases are able to fit together in the confined space thus created. The two polynucleotide chains are the chromatids which we mentioned on page 90, and as we said then, during reproduction they separate so that the newly formed cell has an exact replica of the genetic code contained by its parent. In the new cell the single-stranded DNA chain builds up another replica of itself (in the absence of mutations) so that it will, in turn, be able to pass this code on to its progeny.

We now have to examine the manner in which this coded information of the DNA chain in the nucleus is passed on to the cytoplasm, where the synthesis of the protein molecules takes place in the units called *ribosomes*. Here again, this is a process which is still very much a subject of contemporary research, but it is now generally accepted that the DNA of the nucleus passes its information to the cytoplasm by way of a messenger nucleic acid which differs from DNA in its sugar and is called *ribonucleic acid* (RNA). These RNA molecules are single-stranded poly-nucleotide chains which also carry their information by way of the sequence of their bases and again four different bases are involved, three of which are identical to those of DNA. Thus the RNA polynucleotides act as a 'template' for arranging the sequence of the various amino acids in the ribosomes, giving the enzymes their specificity.

The manner in which the order of the four types of base in the nucleic acid organize the order of the twenty or so amino acids in the protein is only now beginning to be understood. It is suggested that each amino acid is represented by the sequence of three of the four bases. Thus if the four bases are say, A, B, C and D, one amino acid might be represented by the arrangement ABC, another by BDC, and so on. Work on this decoding is still in its very early stages, but it is hoped that it will not be long before the genetic code has been cracked.

It will be observed that, according to this modern theory, the genes, which used to be thought of as separate particles attached to the chromosomes, are no more than a characteristic arrangement of part of the chromosome molecule. This reduction of the 'secrets of life' to a molecular arrangement is taken a step farther in the current views concerning viruses, about which we must now say a few words.

VIRUSES

It has been known since the end of the last century that certain diseases of plants and animals are caused by particles considerably smaller than bacteria, which are only capable of existence and replication inside living cells – these particles are called *viruses*. Viruses are so small (some are only about a millionth of a centimetre in length) that they only became observable after the invention of the electron microscope (see page 178) and their classification has therefore been related to the diseases they cause (e.g., Polio Virus, Tobacco Leaf Mosaic Virus, etc.) rather than to their shape as in the case of bacteria.

Whether or not viruses can be classed as living things is a matter of controversy – they do indeed exhibit many of the characteristics which we have mentioned, but as they are not cellular in construction and as they require a living cell as a host, it is probably safer to regard them as a sort of 'half-way house' between the animate and the inanimate (see page 230). The interesting thing about them is that they have been found to consist of either RNA or DNA molecules encased within a protein, but their infective potency appears to reside entirely with the nucleic acid, for the protein coating may be shed when the virus enters a cell. Once inside a cell a virus is able to replicate itself many times over, and in doing so it destroys its host. It therefore seems that the nucleic acid of the virus in some way usurps the function of the nucleic acid of the cell, thereby disrupting the cellular processes of metabolism and reproduction.

Viruses are very specific about the cells in which they will thrive; only one particular type of cell can serve as a host for a particular type of virus, and it has recently been found that a relationship exists between the order of the bases in the nucleic acid of the virus and that of its host-cell. It appears that the base order of a virus RNA or DNA is exactly the reverse of that of its host's nucleic acids, and it is this fact which may account for the inability of the cell's enzymes to attack the virus.

In conclusion, it is worth noting that certain enzymes have been isolated which catalyse the linking together of individual nucleotides to form RNA or DNA molecules. These reactions can be made to proceed in a test-tube, but the synthetic nucleic acids so created have a random order of bases; so although they may be said to be viruses, no such synthetic virus has yet been created which has the ability to replicate itself in any known cell.

These fascinating experiments are on the very brink of life, and there is little doubt that the intense research that is at present being carried out into the behaviour and constitution of nucleic acids will lead to a new and more profound understanding of the meaning of life in material terms.

PART THREE

ENERGY

CHAPTER 7

THE CONCEPTION OF ENERGY

In the first two parts of this book it has been fairly easy to describe the matter of the universe in terms that can be pictured with reference to our everyday experiences. In doing so, however, it has been necessary to simplify the construction of an atom so that we could visualize it as a miniature solar system consisting of tiny, but solid, particles.

Now that we come to examine the conception of energy more closely it will not always be so easy to depict our ideas with such graphic simplicity, and to some extent our model of the atom will have to be modified by certain considerations which defy visualization. During this part of the book we shall have to accept the fact that electrons, which we have hitherto referred to only as particles, behave also in a manner associated with waves of energy.

By way of consolation it may be said that this difficulty of visualization is not a new experience for mankind. Perhaps our descendants will be as amused at our obtuse grapplings with the idea of particles that behave like waves, as we are at our ancestors for their reluctance to visualize a spherical earth which revolved around the sun.

In describing matter, we referred to its discontinuous nature, and compared it to the continuous quantity – time. From our everyday experiences energy, too, appears to be a continuous quantity, but we shall see when we come to deal with radiant energy, that energy is in fact discontinuous; that is, it increases or decreases by small amounts which have a definite minimum size. The minimum quantity of energy that can exist under given conditions is called a *quantum*, and the theory explaining the discontinuous nature of energy is known as the Quantum Theory.

As these energy quanta are extremely small, it is not necessary to take them into account individually when dealing with the energy associated with large quantities of matter. For example, a spinning top contains a relatively large quantity of matter (compared to an atom) and therefore the energy required to make it spin is very large indeed compared to an energy quantum. Thus, although it is true to say that any increase or decrease in the rate of spin of a top is quantized (i.e., increases or decreases by small jumps), the jumps are so tiny that for all practical purposes the discontinuity can be ignored.

Only when we consider the energy associated with individual atoms or molecules shall we need to consider the Quantum Theory. A gas molecule, for example, has only a tiny mass, therefore the amount of energy required to make it spin like a top is very small – in fact, about the amount contained by an energy quantum. For this reason such a molecule can only spin at certain fixed speeds, any increase or decrease being made in definite jumps; there are therefore certain speeds at which the molecule cannot spin. These considerations will be examined more thoroughly in later chapters.

FORMS OF ENERGY

At this stage we can say that matter is associated with energy in two distinct forms, that is, energy of motion, called *kinetic energy*, and stored energy, called *potential energy*. Each of these two forms of energy contribute to the mass which is the characteristic property of matter. In the case of an electron, part of the mass results from its electric charge (this is the potential energy) and part is contributed by the kinetic energy due to its movement. The greater the speed of movement, the greater the kinetic energy, and consequently the greater the mass (see page 198). In fact an electron moving at 99 per cent of the velocity of light is seven times heavier than an electron at rest. This very great increase of mass with velocity is not an everyday experience because, except at speeds approaching that of light, the increase in mass is so small that it can be ignored. Such speeds, however, are quite common with sub-atomic particles, and in the particle accelerators used in experimental atomic physics this increase of mass with velocity has to be taken into account.

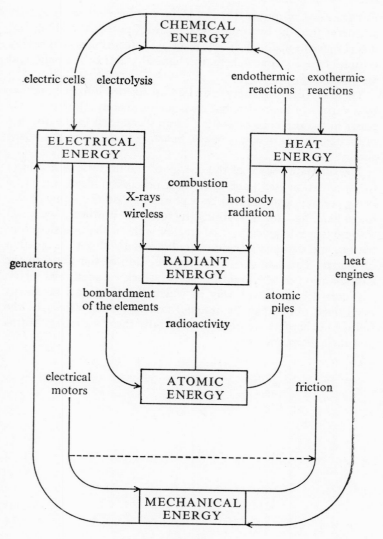

Fig. 19

5

Energy Transformations

For practical purposes it is not always convenient to categorize all energy into the two fundamental forms, potential and kinetic; it is simpler to distinguish between the six forms in which energy is useful to us: chemical, heat, mechanical, electrical, radiant, and atomic energy.

These six forms of energy can be transformed into one another by a variety of processes, but each such transformation can only occur in the presence of matter. Energy can exist in the absence of matter, that is in empty space, but only in the form of radiant energy.

The ultimate source of the energy of the universe is a subject for speculation (see page 224); it is possible, indeed, that it is being continuously created by a power beyond the scope of our understanding. As a working hypothesis, however, we must assume that energy cannot be created without the destruction of matter, and that energy cannot be destroyed without the creation of matter. This statement is a combination of the Laws of the Conservation of Mass and Energy to which we shall refer again.

Figure 19 shows the way in which the six forms of energy mentioned above can be transformed into each other. In the following chapters we discuss more fully these six energy forms and their interconversions.

CHAPTER 8

CHEMICAL ENERGY, HEAT, AND MECHANICAL ENERGY

W E have seen that all matter is composed of atoms or molecules which are in a state of continual movement. These movements include *translation* of the molecule or atom through space (in gases and liquids only), *vibration* of the atoms about fixed positions within the molecule, and, in the case of gases only, *rotation* of the whole molecule. A typical diatomic gas molecule would be subject to the motions shown in Figure 20.

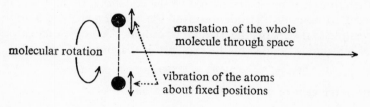

molecular rotation

translation of the whole molecule through space

vibration of the atoms about fixed positions

Fig. 20

These complex motions represent kinetic energy stored within matter (except that the energy of vibration becomes potential energy when the atoms come to rest at the ends of their vibratory movements); potential energy is also stored in the molecules as electrical forces holding the molecule together, and in the form of electronic excitation (see page 189). The total of the kinetic and potential energy so stored within the molecules of matter is called for convenience *chemical energy*. It must be noted that this energy is in addition to the atomic or nuclear energy which is stored within the nucleus of the atom (see page 203).

CHEMICAL ENERGY

As chemical reactions occur when moving molecules collide with each other under appropriate conditions, and as these reactions alter the composition and configuration of the molecules, it is not surprising that all chemical reactions are accompanied by a change in the energy-content of the reacting system. This change of energy-content is due to the redistribution of the chemical energy only – the atomic energy remains totally unchanged by chemical reactions.

Exothermic and Endothermic Reactions

If the redistribution of energy during a chemical reaction is such that the energy of the reacting atoms or molecules is greater than that of the products, then the excess of energy is given off as heat energy or radiant energy, and the reaction is said to be *exothermic*. On the other hand, if heat energy has to be supplied to the reacting system by the surroundings, the reaction is called *endothermic*. In order to specify a chemical reaction completely, therefore, it is necessary to add to the equations which we have used to describe the quantities of the reacting matter, a term relating to the energy (heat) input or output. A complete equation of reaction is typified by the exothermic reaction:

$$2H_2 + O_2 = 2H_2O + 3{,}200 \text{ calories per gram}$$

or in the case of an endothermic reaction:

$$2C + H_2 = C_2H_2 - 2{,}100 \text{ calories per gram}$$

From these examples it will be seen that the formation of one gram of water is accompanied by the evolution of 3,200 calories of heat energy, while the formation of one gram of acetylene (C_2H_2) requires the addition of 2,100 calories of heat from the surroundings.

We have already explained that energy can only be created by a system at the expense of the quantity of matter which it contains. It is therefore to be expected that when hydrogen and oxygen combine to form water with the evolution of heat energy, the mass of water formed will be less than the combined mass of the reactants (oxygen and hydrogen). This is in fact the case, but, as we have already pointed out, a very great deal of energy is required to make even a tiny quantity of matter. In the above example, the amount of matter that is lost in order to create 3,200 calories of heat is less than one thousand millionth part of a gram of water. Such a quantity of matter is immeasurably small, so we may say, to a very close approximation, that the mass of a reacting system remains constant if chemical energy only is involved. (This is the Law of Conservation of Mass referred to on page 130.) However, if atomic energy is liberated this approximation does not hold as the mass associated with the energy liberated by the disintegration of an atomic nucleus is of the same order of magnitude as the mass of the atom itself (see Chapter 11).

The Calorie

In the foregoing examples we have used the unit of heat energy called a *calorie*, which must now be explained. A calorie is simply the amount of heat required to raise the temperature of one gram of water by one degree Centigrade. This is quite a small quantity of heat – the average domestic kettle holds about 1,000 grams of water, therefore to raise it to boiling-point (i.e., to increase its temperature by, say, 85°C, from 15°C to 100°C) requires 85 × 1,000 = 85,000 calories. (This calculation ignores the heat required to raise the temperature of the container and the heat that is lost to the surroundings.) The Calories used for calculating our food intake are a thousand times larger and are spelt with a capital 'C' to distinguish them.

HEAT ENERGY

We have seen how chemical energy is converted into heat energy by an exothermic chemical reaction, and conversely how heat energy goes to make up the chemical energy in an endothermic reaction. In order to explain what this heat energy is it will be necessary to distinguish between heat and temperature.

In discussing the physical states of matter we saw that temperature was a measure of the kinetic energy of the moving atoms or molecules comprising matter. Thus, a very small quantity of matter can have a very high temperature. On the other hand, the heat energy possessed by a body is related to its temperature and to the number and kind of atoms or molecules of which it is constructed. That is to say, the heat contained by a body depends not only on its temperature but also on its mass.

Therefore a very heavy body can be at a low temperature but still contain a large amount of heat.

An incandescent speck of hot metal from a grindstone does not burn our skin although it has a high temperature, because it has too little mass to contain much heat. In contrast, St Thomas's Hospital, London, is heated by the water of the River Thames. Owing to the hot effluents from factories that are pumped into the river along its course, the temperature of the water in London is very slightly above that of the surroundings: as millions of tons of water flow through London daily, plenty of 'low temperature' heat is available. A machine called a 'heat pump' is used to raise the temperature of this heat so that it can be usefully employed to warm the hospital.

In making this point about a heat pump, it must be stressed that in order to be able to extract useful energy from a source of heat, it must be at a higher temperature than its surroundings. It is not possible, for example, to use the heat of the ocean to drive a ship, because the sea would never be at a higher temperature than the ship. This fact, that heat will never flow from one source to another at a higher temperature (without the application of energy from an outside source) is the basis of an important law called the Second Law of Thermodynamics.

The Laws of Thermodynamics

At this point it may be appropriate to say a word about thermodynamics, which, as its name implies, is the study of the flow of heat or energy. This science is based on three fundamental laws, which, being statistical in nature, can only be applied to large numbers of atoms or molecules – we have already seen that statistical laws do not apply to individuals.

The First Law of Thermodynamics states that energy can be neither created nor destroyed, and is also known as the Law of Conservation of Energy. This law, and the Law of Conservation of Mass (see page 133) have been combined into Einstein's Law of the Equivalence of Mass and Energy (see page 198). We must now say, therefore, that the First Law of Thermodynamics applies only to systems of constant mass. The Second Law of Thermodynamics, which we have mentioned in the last paragraph, we shall refer to again on page 137 when we discuss entropy; at the same time we shall refer to the Third Law.

Combustion

If a reaction is strongly exothermic and proceeds very rapidly, the process is called *combustion*. Nearly all combustion reactions are oxidation reactions (see page 51) in which the oxygen is supplied by the atmosphere.

Most of the energy required by our civilization is derived from the heat energy obtained by the combustion of the fossil fuels (coal, oil, and natural gas). As the chemical energy of these fuels is stored in molecules consisting mostly of carbon and hydrogen, the two most important combustion reactions are the oxidation of carbon to carbon dioxide:

$$C + O_2 = CO_2 + 2,100 \text{ calories per gram}$$

and the familiar oxidation of hydrogen to water:

$$2H_2 + O_2 = 2H_2O + 3,200 \text{ calories per gram}$$

Other reactions occur, as there are other elements present to a small extent in the fossil fuels, but these two are by far the most important in calculating the total heat energy which will be evolved when coal or oil are burned.

The nitrogen in the air (air is three-quarters nitrogen) takes no part in the combustion process, and is therefore present in the products of combustion together with water (as steam) and carbon dioxide. Its presence has the effect of reducing the temperature and the available energy of a combustion reaction, so that if pure oxygen is used instead of air much higher temperatures result.

MECHANICAL ENERGY

In Figure 19 on page 129 showing the energy conversions that take place in the presence of matter, we saw that heat energy is converted into mechanical energy by a heat engine (for example a steam, petrol, or Diesel piston engine, or a steam or gas turbine). Conversely, the mechanical movement of one piece of matter on, or through, another causes friction which results in some part of the mechanical energy being converted into heat.

If we think again of matter as being composed of rapidly moving atoms or molecules, we can appreciate that the conversion of heat energy into mechanical energy, for example in the cylinder of a piston engine, comes about as a result of the random motions of the gas molecules imparting to the atoms of the metal piston an overall uniform motion in one direction. The piston, being a solid free to move in one direction only, acquires its kinetic energy as a result of the impact of those gas molecules which collide with it. Thus the conversion of heat into mechanical energy is a way of organizing and making use of the random kinetic energy of moving molecules. It should be made clear that mechanical energy is a form of kinetic energy, but it is kinetic energy which is directed to some mechanical purpose.

In the case of friction, the opposite is the case. For example, some of the organized mechanical energy of a rotating shaft goes to increase the disorganized vibrations of the metal atoms of the bearing through which it runs; this increased vibrational energy of the metal atoms means that its temperature is raised and the bearing therefore becomes heated as a result of the friction.

Entropy

This loss of energy through friction is only one example of a more general phenomenon. It is an observed fact (though not a theoretical one) that throughout the universe energy tends to be dissipated in such a way that the total available energy becomes more disorganized and more difficult to trap and use.

One only has to think of driving down the road in a car. The chemical energy stored in the petrol is converted into heat by combustion and then into mechanical energy in the engine. The organized mechanical energy so produced results in the controlled and organized motion of the car. But some of that energy has been irrevocably dissipated in heating the road as a result of the friction of the tyres, heating the air with the exhaust gases, and by overcoming wind resistance. This energy is lost to us for good.

The extent to which energy is in a state of disorganization is measured by a quantity called *entropy*. The higher the state of disorganization the higher the entropy – the lower the extent of disorganization the lower the entropy. In fact, as the Third Law of Thermodynamics states, at the Absolute Zero of Temperature (see page 47) when all atomic vibration and motion stops, the entropy is zero, because there is no disorganized motion.

In the preceding paragraphs we have said that it is an observed fact that the total energy of the universe tends to become more disorganized, and consequently we may say that the entropy of the universe is always increasing. This is another way of expressing the Second Law of Thermodynamics which, it will be remembered, states that heat will not flow from a cold to a hot body without the application of external energy (see page 134).

Thus, should the universe finally unwind itself completely, so that every part of it is at the same temperature, there would be no energy available for use. This would be the ultimate state of the disorganization of energy, because all molecular and atomic motions would be at random, and, in accordance with the Second Law of Thermodynamics, they would be unable to impart a uniform motion to other atoms of matter. Were this to happen the entropy of the universe would be at its maximum.

This condition, which is referred to as the 'Heat Death of the Universe', has been of great interest to philosophers as well as scientists. For if the universe can in fact be regarded as a closed system subject to the Second Law of Thermodynamics (which is by no means certain), it not only follows that it will have a finite end, but also that it had a finite beginning; for if it had been created an infinite time ago it would by now have inevitably suffered its heat death. We shall refer to the creation of the universe again in greater detail in Chapter 12.

Efficiency of Mechanical Systems

The inevitable wastage of available energy due to friction, loss of heat to the surroundings, etc., when heat is converted into mechanical energy, has given engineers cause to express the proportion of energy that is available for useful work as the *efficiency* of the system. The efficiency is defined simply as the percentage of 'possible energy' that can be extracted as 'useful energy' from a system. For example, the efficiency of a petrol engine is about 20 per cent, that is to say, for every gallon of petrol burnt in the engine which contains a possible heat energy of about 30 million calories, only 6 million calories are available for driving the car. Of the remaining 80 per cent, about three-eighths are carried away by the cooling water and five-eighths lost as heat from the exhaust gases and friction in the bearings.

By comparison with these figures, when electrical energy is converted into mechanical energy in an electric motor the efficiency is far greater, and for really big machines can be as high as 95 per cent.

CHAPTER 9

ELECTRICAL ENERGY

In the previous chapter reactions were described in which chemical energy was converted into heat energy. In certain reactions, now to be outlined, chemical energy can be converted directly into electrical energy.

THE ELECTRIC CELL

As will be seen in Figure 21, such reactions take place in a so-called *electric cell*, the simplest form of which is made by dipping a rod of zinc (Zn) and a rod of copper (Cu) into a solution of sulphuric acid (H_2SO_4) in water.

The zinc dissolves in the acid forming zinc ions, sulphate ions, and hydrogen ions; so, using the symbols given on page 49 and 'e' to depict an electron, the equation of reaction may be written thus:

$$2Zn + H_2SO_4 \rightarrow 2Zn^+ + SO_4'' + 2H^+ + 2e$$

For every two zinc ions that go into solution, two electrons are left behind on the zinc rod. If a piece of metal wire is connected between the exposed ends of the zinc and copper rods these electrons will flow through the wire into the copper rod; this flow of electrons constitutes an electric current. The flow of electrons to the copper rod will cause it to become negatively charged, and it will therefore attract the positively charged hydrogen ions which will consequently collect around it. The excess of electrons contained by the copper rod will unite with the hydrogen ions to form atoms of hydrogen which will be liberated as diatomic gas molecules around the copper rod. The metal rods in a cell are called the *electrodes*, and the liquid in which they are immersed is called the *electrolyte*.

It will be noticed from the above description that the copper electrode does not enter into the reaction; but the choice of the

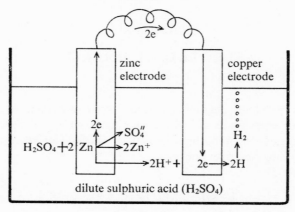

Fig. 21

metal of which the electrode is made is important because different metals will produce different quantities of electrical energy. Not only can various metals be used, but a variety of electrolytes are also possible, so that a large number of different cells can be devised for producing electricity. The simple form of cell described above has certain practical disadvantages, but in a modified form it is widely used in 'dry' batteries.

Cells in which chemical energy is converted into electrical energy are called *primary cells*, while cells in which electrical energy is stored in the form of chemical energy, as for example the lead accumulator, are called *secondary cells*.

Nearly all the reactions which occur in an electric cell are reversible. That is to say, the introduction of electrical energy into the cell will make the reaction go backwards. This reverse process, known as *electrolysis*, is used for coating one metal with another. Gold, silver, chromium, and tin are among the metals that are commercially plated on to cheaper metals in this way.

Electric Potential, Current, and Resistance
If the wire joining the electrodes of a primary cell is cut the chemical reaction will cease, but there will exist between the electrodes a potential force which is capable of producing energy if the wire is joined again. This is called an *electro-motive force* and

it is measured in units called *volts*. The cell described above has an electro-motive force of 1·1 volts.

The number of electrons which flow through the wire in a given time is, of course, a measure of the quantity of electricity flowing, and this quantity is called the *current* which is measured in *amperes*. As a rough guide, the number of electrons which are required to light an electric lamp is about one million, million, million per second.

The current which will flow through a wire, or any other conductor of electricity, depends on the force available to drive the electrons (i.e., the potential) and the *resistance* of the conductor. The resistance of a wire depends on the material of which it is made, its length, and its thickness. Obviously the thicker and shorter the wire, the lower its resistance. The resistance to the flow of electrons in any material can be simply measured and the unit of resistance is the *ohm*.

Ohm's Law

The three electrical units mentioned in the preceding paragraph, the volt, the ampere, and the ohm, have been so chosen that a potential of 1 volt will drive a current of 1 ampere through a resistance of 1 ohm.

Furthermore, there is a simple law, called Ohm's Law after its formulator, relating these three quantities: namely that the voltage (V) is equal to the product of the resistance (R) and the current (I), or in symbols: $V = IR$.

Energy of an Electric Current

The energy that is available from an electric current is equal to the product of the current in amperes, the time for which it flows, and the voltage that drives it. The unit of electrical energy is called the watt-hour (Wh); thus a current of 1 ampere flowing for 1 hour at a potential of 1 volt will produce 1 watt-hour of electrical energy.

When a current is passed through a wire, the wire is heated as a result of the passage of electrons, and the heat energy so generated can be used for a variety of purposes – heating the water in an electric kettle, for example. It will be remembered that in the last chapter we said that the heat energy required to bring an average-size kettle to the boil is about 85,000 calories. As 1 watt-hour of electrical energy is equivalent to 860 calories of heat energy, we see that an average kettle would require just less than 100 watt-hours to bring its contents to the boil. In the London area the cost of 1,000 watt-hours (1 kilowatt-hour) is about 1*d*., so that boiling a kettle should cost about $\frac{1}{10}d$. In practice the cost will be slightly more because some of the heat will be lost to the surroundings.

ELECTRIC FIELDS

We have shown in the last paragraphs how the movement of electrons constitutes an electric current, but so far we have not mentioned static electric charges which are also a familiar every-day experience. For example, if a poor conductor of electricity, such as amber or sealing wax, is rubbed with a silk cloth, the amber develops the power of attracting a small piece of matter such as a slip of paper. In this condition, a non-conductor is said to be charged with electricity. The mechanism of this charging process is that the rubbing motion strips the outside atoms of the amber of some of their electrons, so that at the surface of the material there is a residual positive electric charge. This positive charge exerts an attractive force on the electrons in the atoms of the paper, and consequently the paper adheres to the amber.

If this simple experiment is carried out, it will be observed that the amber or sealing wax does not actually have to touch the paper before the attraction begins. The attractive force has the ability to bridge a small gap; in this gap there is said to be an *electric field* across which energy can be transmitted. In general, an electric field exists between any two charged particles of matter, and, as we shall learn, the transference of energy by an electric field in space is a most important conception in modern physics. This field is closely related to a magnetic field.

MAGNETIC FIELDS

Magnetic fields are familiar in association with bar and horseshoe magnets, which have the power of attracting small pieces of iron.

If a bar magnet is placed on a sheet of paper, on which tiny pieces of iron filings have been sprinkled, the direction of the magnetic forces can be directly observed by tapping the paper gently so that the filings arrange themselves along the so-called *lines of force* of the magnet, as in Figure 22. The area over which these lines of force act is called the *magnetic field*, and again, as with electric fields, energy is transmitted through space.

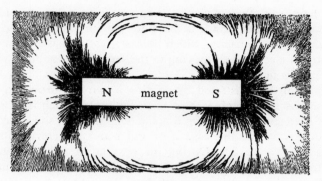

Fig. 22

The nature of these magnetic forces is still to a large extent unexplained, although it is known that a single spinning electron will create a similar field on a miniature scale. It has also been shown that in a magnetized bar of iron the electrons are all spinning in the same direction, whereas in a non-magnetized bar the direction of electron-spin is at random. However, there is no satisfactory explanation as to why some conductors make better magnets than others, although this connexion between electrically charged particles and magnetic forces forms the basis of the whole theory of electro-magnetic radiation.

It must be added that a freely pivoted bar magnet will always adopt a definite position with respect to the earth, such that one end points in the general direction of the North Pole and the other in the direction of the South Pole. This behaviour, which is of course the basis of the magnetic compass, occurs because the direction of the lines of force of the magnet strive to coincide with the direction of the lines of force of the earth's magnetic field. For convenience it is usual to refer to the north-seeking end of a magnet as its north pole, and its south-seeking end as its south pole. It is also a familiar experience that like magnetic poles repel each other and unlike poles attract each other, behaving in this respect in exactly the same manner as electric charges.

Magnetic Effect of an Electric Current

We have said that a single spinning electron behaves like a miniature magnet, and it is therefore not surprising to find that a current of electricity, which consists, as we have seen, of a stream of electrons all moving in the same direction, also exerts a magnetic field.

This can be illustrated by sending a current through a wire which passes through a sheet of paper on to which iron filings have been sprinkled. Again, tapping the paper will show the lines of force, which in this case are circular and concentric with the wire (see Figure 23). During the passage of the current, the electrons all spin in the same direction, but when the current ceases to flow the direction of the spins returns to a random distribution, and consequently the magnetic field dies.

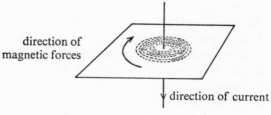

direction of
magnetic forces

direction of current

Fig. 23

If the piece of wire carrying the current is formed into a coil, the circular lines of force round the wire combine to produce a magnetic field which is somewhat similar to that produced by a bar magnet. This arrangement, which is called an *electro-magnet*, is illustrated in Figure 24.

If a soft iron core is now inserted through the coil of wire, and an arrangement is made for switching the current on and off

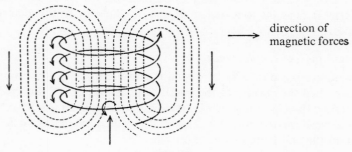

Fig. 24

rapidly, the core will become alternately magnetized and de-magnetized so that it will alternately attract and release a light piece of iron. If the piece of iron is pivoted at one end and fitted with a spring it can be made to vibrate in the changing magnetic field. This is the principle of the electromagnetic bell, as illustrated in Figure 25. It will be noticed that the trembler itself is used to switch the current on and off by making and breaking the circuit from the cell to the coil.

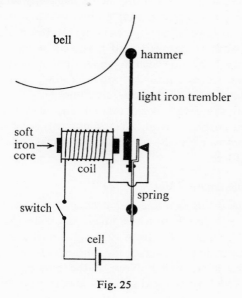

Fig. 25

This principle of obtaining mechanical energy from electrical energy is brought to a higher degree of efficiency in the electric motor.

Electromagnetic Induction

If another piece of wire is looped round a coil, it will be found that, when the current to the coil is switched on or off, a current will flow through the loop of wire. This latter current is said to be an *induced current*, and it will occur only when the magnetic field round the coil is in a state of change.

Another way of inducing a current, is to move a length of wire physically across a magnetic field so that it cuts the magnetic lines of force. This method is the principle of the dynamo, which consists essentially of a coil of wire rotating in a magnetic field. In this way the lines of force of the magnet are being cut by the rotating coil and a current is therefore developed in the coil. Thus the mechanical energy used to rotate the coil in the magnetic field is converted into electrical energy within the coil. The dynamo, or generator as larger machines are usually called, is one of the most economical methods of producing electricity on a large scale, and it is this method that is adopted in power stations.

The exact reverse of a dynamo is the electric motor, in which the coil of wire is supplied with a current which is broken at regular intervals by a device known as a commutator; the resulting magnetic forces cause the coil to rotate, so that electrical energy is transformed into mechanical energy.

In general, then, we may say that any movement of an electrically charged particle, or any electric current, creates a magnetic force, and conversely any movement of a magnetic pole creates an electric force.

The Electromagnetic Field

We can extend this example of an induced current to the circuit illustrated in Figure 26 in which an electric cell supplies a stream of electrons to a coil of wire, A, through a switch, S. This switch is so arranged that it reverses the connexions of the cell to the coil A when it is rotated. Now, if the switch is continuously rotated by some mechanical means, the current in the coil A will be constantly and regularly changing in direction. The field created by the constantly changing current is called an *electro-magnetic field*, and it will surround the coil A.

If a second and similar coil of wire, B, is placed within this field, a constantly changing current will be induced in this coil, so that if an instrument for measuring current is placed across its ends the needle will swing backwards and forwards, indicating first a negative and then a positive current, depending on the position of the switch S. Such a current which regularly changes

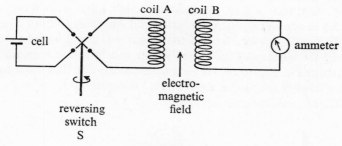

Fig. 26

direction is called an *alternating current*, although the current produced from the apparatus shown would not be 'pure'. However, if we used a switch which gradually increased, decreased, and reversed the current in coil A and then took measurements of the current in coil B at very frequent intervals, and plotted them on a graph (Figure 27), we should find that the current

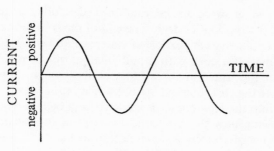

Fig. 27

would change from positive to negative in a smooth and regular manner. This is a typical wave-form, which is characteristic of the way in which energy is radiated from one piece of matter (coil A) to another (coil B) by an electromagnetic field in space.

In general, any oscillating current, or any vibrating electric charge, will produce the sort of electromagnetic field which we have described, and energy will be transmitted through the field, in the form of waves, at a definite speed which will be discussed on page 149. As it is not easy to visualize how energy can be transmitted by these electromagnetic waves, an analogy may help. Consider a long glass-sided trough filled with water, in which at one end a pencil is inserted and vigorously vibrated back and forth. The vibrations of the pencil will cause waves to run along the surface of the water which will have the appearance illustrated in Figure 28 – if we are able to assume that the trough is sufficiently long to be able to avoid the complications of waves reflected from the ends.

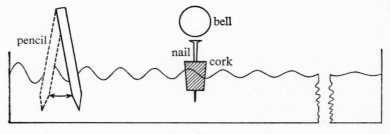

Fig. 28

If the water were to be examined carefully, it would be observed that no motion from one end of the trough to the other was taking place; each particle of water would be simply moving up or down. If a cork with a nail sticking out of it were to be floated in the water in the middle of the trough, it would be found that the cork bobbed up and down in the waves. The nail sticking into the cork could be made to hit a bell on its upstroke, thus showing how the mechanical energy of the moving pencil could be transferred by a wave-motion to the cork, where some of it is used again as mechanical energy in ringing a bell.

This analogy breaks down badly over the question of the medium through which the waves are radiated. In the trough the waves are supported in the medium of the water, in the case of electromagnetic waves, no medium whatsoever is required. In our example of the two coils A and B, both could have been housed in a container from which all the air had been evacuated. Although it is not easy to visualize, it must be accepted that electromagnetic waves can travel through empty space.

Electromagnetic Waves

It is now necessary to return to an examination of the characteristics of the electromagnetic waves themselves. The two chief characteristics of a wave are its *amplitude* and its *wave-length*

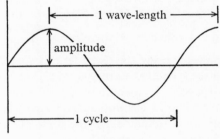

Fig. 29

(Figure 29). The amplitude, or height, is a measure of the amount of energy it contains (the energy is actually proportional to the *square* of the amplitude) while its wave-length determines its nature. Very long electromagnetic waves (several hundreds of metres) are those used in ordinary sound broadcasting; very short waves, as will be explained in the next chapter, transfer energy to which our eyes are sensitive – that is to say they are light waves.

It has already been mentioned that electromagnetic waves travel at a definite speed – this speed does not depend on the wave-length, and is the same for all electromagnetic radiations. For historical reasons it is usually referred to as the 'velocity of light', although it would be more correct to speak of the 'velocity of electromagnetic radiation'.

We shall show later that the velocity of light has a special significance in the universe (see page 194); for the moment we will simply give its value, which is 186,000 miles per second, or 300 million metres per second. Slight variations in this velocity occur depending on the medium through which the waves are travelling; the figures given represent the velocity in space. It is not always convenient to refer to a wave's length, because this will vary with the speed of the wave and will change if the wave passes from one medium to another. It is, therefore, often preferable to refer to the *frequency* with which a cycle (i.e., a complete wave-length) is repeated. It is a simple mathematical calculation to show that the number of cycles per second, which is called the frequency of the wave, is equal to the speed at which the wave is travelling, divided by its wave-length. We are, of course, familiar with both these terms when we tune our radios. For example, the wave-length of the London Home Service of the BBC is 330 metres, and the frequency is therefore $\frac{300,000,000}{330} = 908,000$ cycles per second, or, using the usual term, *kilocycle* (i.e., 1,000 cycles), 330 metres is equivalent to 908 kilocycles per second.

In Table 4 (page 151) the full range of wave-lengths and frequencies for all known electromagnetic waves are given. The study of each group of frequencies is the study of radiant energy, which forms the subject-matter of the next chapter.

Very Large and Small Numbers

It will have become apparent during the course of this book that in science it is often necessary to refer both to very large and very small numbers. When dealing with the full range of frequencies and wave-lengths of electromagnetic radiations this problem becomes particularly acute, and for such purposes it would be extremely cumbersome to have to speak of millions of millions of cycles or million millionths of metres. It would be equally inconvenient to have recourse to rows of noughts either before or after the significant figures.

To overcome this difficulty a very simple notation is used in which the number of noughts which follow or precede the significant figures are indicated by raising 10 to the appropriate power, for example:

Table 4

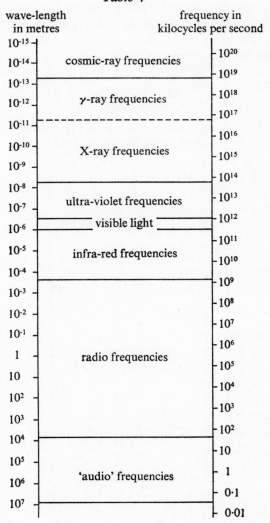

wave-length in metres		frequency in kilocycles per second
10^{-15}		
10^{-14}	cosmic-ray frequencies	10^{20}
		10^{19}
10^{-13}		
10^{-12}	γ-ray frequencies	10^{18}
		10^{17}
10^{-11}		
		10^{16}
10^{-10}	X-ray frequencies	
		10^{15}
10^{-9}		
		10^{14}
10^{-8}		
10^{-7}	ultra-violet frequencies	10^{13}
	visible light	10^{12}
10^{-6}		
		10^{11}
10^{-5}	infra-red frequencies	
		10^{10}
10^{-4}		
10^{-3}		10^{9}
		10^{8}
10^{-2}		
		10^{7}
10^{-1}		
		10^{6}
1	radio frequencies	
		10^{5}
10		
		10^{4}
10^{2}		
		10^{3}
10^{3}		
		10^{2}
10^{4}		
		10
10^{5}		
	'audio' frequencies	1
10^{6}		
		0·1
10^{7}		
		0·01

$$10^1 = 10$$
$$10^2 = 100$$
$$10^3 = 1,000$$

and so forth. Thus, $10^6 = 1$ million and $10^{12} = 1$ million million. Using this notation, the number 5,420,000 would be written $5 \cdot 42 \times 10^6$.

On the same principle:

$$10^{-1} = 1/10 = 0 \cdot 1$$
$$10^{-2} = 1/100 = 0 \cdot 01$$
$$10^{-6} = 1 \text{ millionth}$$

Thus, four millionths would be written $4 \cdot 0 \times 10^{-6}$.

This notation will be used throughout the rest of the book.

CHAPTER 10

RADIANT ENERGY

IN the previous chapter we have shown how energy can be radiated through space in the form of electromagnetic waves, which are created by the oscillation or vibration of an electric charge or collection of charges. It has also been explained that the properties of these waves depend on their frequencies, which can vary from about 20 cycles per second to about 10^{24} cycles per second.

We now come to study the sources which produce these oscillations and the properties that characterize each group of frequencies. For convenience we will start at the lower end of the frequency scale and work our way upwards.

RADIO FREQUENCY WAVES

Radio frequency waves fall within the frequency band 20 cycles per second to 10^7 kilocycles per second (i.e. 10^{10} cycles per second), and are all produced by the oscillation of a current of electrons in specially designed circuits, the principles of which we shall shortly outline. Radio waves, however, are themselves subdivided into several groups according to wave-length or frequency, as in Table 5.

Table 5

	Wave-length in metres	*Frequency, kilocycles per second*
Audio frequencies	Over 10,000	Below 30
Long and medium wave	10,000–100	30–3,000
Short wave	100–10	3,000–30,000
Very high frequency	10–1	30,000–3×10^5
Ultra high frequency	1–0·1	3×10^5–3×10^6
Radar frequency	0·1–0·01	3×10^6–3×10^7

The lowest frequencies are called audio frequencies because they correspond to the frequencies of sound waves to which our ears are sensitive. It will therefore be necessary to digress briefly on the subject of the transmission of energy by sound waves, although these are not, of course, electromagnetic waves.

SOUND WAVES

If a stretched wire or string is plucked, it will vibrate in a regular manner at a definite frequency which will depend on the thickness and material of the string, its tension, and its unsupported length.

The energy of the vibrating string will cause the surrounding molecules of air to vibrate in a similar manner, so that a sound-wave will be transmitted in all directions through the air with a frequency identical to that of the vibrating string. This wave, when it impinges on the ear-drum, will cause a vibration to pass through the bone and nerves of the inner ear to the brain. The ear, being a very delicate instrument, is capable of differentiating between frequencies in the whole range of audibility, and the brain will register that a certain note has been sounded. The range of human audibility is from about 20 cycles per second to about 20,000 cycles per second (although with advancing age the upper limit becomes somewhat reduced), and any periodic vibration of matter, in any form, within this frequency range will cause an audible sound.

All sounds have three characteristics, namely: *pitch*, *loudness*, and *quality* (or *timbre*).

The *pitch* of a sound depends solely on its frequency: a pure musical note consists of one basic frequency; for example, middle C on the piano has a basic frequency of 256 cycles per second. Doubling the frequency produces a note one octave higher, and the musical scale is developed by dividing the octave into twelve approximately equal intervals.

The *loudness* of a sound depends on the amount of energy contained by the wave by which it is transmitted and is related directly to its amplitude.

The *quality* or *timbre* of a sound depends on the number and strength of the overtones which are produced together with the basic frequency. In the example of the stretched string we said that the string vibrates at a fixed frequency, dependent, amongst other things, on its length. A string, or a vibrating column of air, however, has the ability of dividing itself into two, three, four, or more parts, each part itself vibrating at a frequency character-istic of the divided length. The notes so produced are called overtones, and they are distinguishable, by a trained musician, from the basic note. Every source of sound will have a character-istic quality depending upon the extent to which these overtones are produced. It is for this reason that, say, a piano and a clarinet produce differing sounds at the same pitch (i.e. the same frequency).

The transmission of energy in the form of sound waves has very much in common with the transmission of energy by electro-magnetic waves, but there are three important differences. Firstly, sound waves cannot be radiated through empty space – they require matter for their propagation (solid, liquid, or gaseous). Secondly, they travel much more slowly than electromagnetic waves; the speed of sound depends on the material through which it is passing, being faster in solids than in liquids, and faster in liquids than in gases; but, as an example, the velocity of sound in air (at sea-level) is about 740 miles per hour, which is of course slower than our fastest (supersonic) aeroplanes.

The third difference between sound and electromagnetic waves is that the former are longitudinal waves, whereas the latter are transverse waves. This statement requires a few words of explanation. In a transverse wave the undulations are at right angles to the direction of the wave; in the glass-sided trough, mentioned in the last chapter (page 148), the cork bobbed up and down in the vertical plane, while the wave was travelling in the horizontal plane. This is a typical transverse wave and electro-magnetic waves are of this type. In a longitudinal wave, however, the movement of the particles is back and forth, in the same direction as the wave, not across it as with a transverse wave. This means that a sound-wave in air consists of alternating regions of pressure and rarefaction progressing along the wave.

The Conversion of Sound into Electric Currents

Sound waves can be converted into electric currents by a microphone, the simplest type of which consists of an arrangement very similar to the electric bell which we have already described in the last chapter. In this kind of microphone, however, the trembler of the bell is replaced by a thin metal diaphragm which is firmly secured round its edges. When the sound waves impinge on this diaphragm it is caused to vibrate, and therefore to cut the lines of force of the electro-magnet (see Figure 30) at exactly the frequency of the impinging sound. The current thereby induced in the coil of the electro-magnet will also oscillate at the frequency of the original sound, and can be led through a wire to any desired destination, where it can be re-created as a sound wave by an exactly similar process in reverse. This is the principle of the telephone.

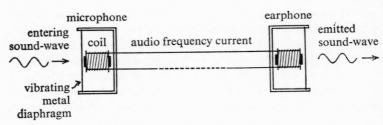

Fig. 30

The microphone shown in this figure is of the simplest type; better quality instruments employ different techniques to achieve the same end. In this example, the current has been re-created as a sound wave by a metal diaphragm, which is only suitable for reproducing a small volume of sound. To create sound waves of greater volume and fidelity a loudspeaker is required, which consists essentially of a similar arrangement to the earphone, except that the metal diaphragm is replaced by a vibrating paper cone. As a loudspeaker causes a far greater quantity of air to vibrate it requires greater energy for its operation, and therefore an amplifier is required in the circuit.

Electronic Amplifiers

Electronic amplifiers are based either on the *electronic valve* or on the *transistor*; the mode of operation of the former is described below and illustrated in Figure 31.

If two wires from a high-voltage battery (a collection of electric cells joined together) are sealed into a glass tube so that their ends are separated by an air space, no current will flow between the wires because the electrons cannot escape from the surface of the metal of the wire. If, however, the wire connected to the negative terminal of the battery is heated to red heat, and the air is removed from the tube, the electrons will break free from the metal and will collect in a cloud around the negative wire (which is called the *cathode*). As the other wire is connected to the positive terminal of the battery, this wire (which is called the *anode*) will become positively charged, and will therefore attract the 'free' electrons liberated by the cathode. A current of electrons will then flow from the cathode to the anode. It should be noted that this device will only allow current to flow in the one direction, and it is for this reason that it is known in Britain as a valve.

If a wire gauze is inserted into the glass tube and fixed into position between the two electrodes, the electrons will have to flow through this gauze (which is called the *grid*). If the grid is negatively charged it will repel the negative electrons emitted by the cathode, and the current will cease to flow to the anode. If, on the other hand, the grid is made positively charged, but less so than the anode, it will attract the electrons and accelerate them on their path to the anode, thus increasing the current flowing through the valve.

It can be appreciated, therefore, that by choosing a suitable fixed grid voltage (or *bias* as it is called) the flow of current can be controlled by small fluctuations in voltage superimposed on this grid bias. Thus, if a weak oscillating current is fed into a suitably biased grid, a similar oscillation of greater amplitude will be reproduced in the main current flowing from the cathode to the anode. The energy output of the anode-cathode circuit can be made very large by suitable valve design and circuit characteristics, as it is not dependent on the energy-input to the grid. In

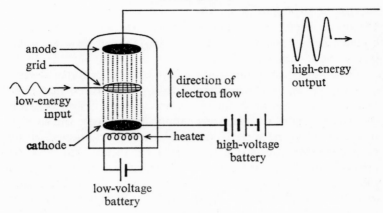

Fig. 31

this way a weak grid current can be amplified into a strong anode current, so that if the output of a microphone is fed into the grid of such a valve sufficient energy might be produced at the anode to operate a loudspeaker. Greater amplification can of course be produced by using two or more such valves in series. The valve described above contains three electrodes and is therefore called a *triode*; more powerfully amplifying valves can also be used containing four electrodes (*tetrodes*) or five electrodes (*pentodes*).

Transistors, also used as electronic amplifiers, make use of the characteristics of very pure crystals of certain substances to conduct electricity in one direction only under certain conditions. By using a sandwich of three such semi-conductor crystals, the centre layer may be made to act like the grid in the electronic valve and amplification can be achieved on a similar principle. Transistors have the advantage over valves that they are much smaller and lighter, and furthermore they do not need to be heated in order to produce a flow of electrons.

Broadcasting Electromagnetic Waves

We have seen how sound waves can be transformed into electric currents, and how these currents can be amplified. We now come to consider the transmission, or broadcasting, of electromagnetic waves over long distances.

For a variety of reasons, it is not practicable to transmit radio waves of very low frequencies – for one thing the transmitting aerial would have to be impossibly large. It is therefore not possible to broadcast electromagnetic waves of audio frequencies, and for long-distance transmission it is necessary to resort to higher frequencies and therefore shorter wave-lengths; the wave-lengths actually used vary from about 1 metre to 2,000 metres. (See Table 5 on p. 153.)

In general, electromagnetic waves of radio frequency are propagated through the earth's atmosphere in two ways; namely, *ground waves* which travel over the surface of the earth, and *sky waves*, which leave the surface of the earth and are reflected back by ionized layers of the outer atmosphere between 60 and 400 miles above the earth's surface. This ionized region of the atmosphere is called the *ionosphere* and is divided into layers, two of which are known as the *Heaviside-Kennelly layer* and the *Appleton layer* after their discoverers.

The ionization of the atoms and molecules in the ionosphere is largely caused by the action of the ultra-violet radiation (see page 185) from the sun, and therefore the conditions for reflecting sky waves vary from day to night. After sunset the degree of ionization in the lower (Heaviside) layer falls off due to the re-combination of ions, and reflection is then effected by the higher (Appleton) layer, which being less dense (fewer collisions occurring between ions and electrons) remains ionized for longer periods. Figure 32 illustrates the two methods of transmission.

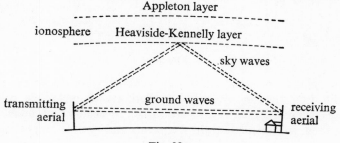

Fig. 32

Long waves (in the radio-frequency band) are transmitted as ground waves and therefore lose a good deal of their energy in passing through ground obstacles; they consequently have only a limited range. The shorter waves, however, escape more easily from the surface of the earth and can be received over greater distances owing to their reflection back to the earth by the ionosphere. Very short waves pass through the ionosphere so they cannot be used for long-distance communications. This is why the range of TV stations is limited.

Modulation

We have explained that, for long-distance radio transmission, frequencies far in excess of audio frequencies have to be used and, therefore, in order to transmit sound by radio, a combination of the transmitting frequency and the audio frequency has to be arranged. This can be achieved by controlling, or *modulating*, the amplitude of the high-frequency wave (called the *carrier*) in accordance with the frequency of the sound wave. This process is called *amplitude modulation* and is illustrated in Figure 33.

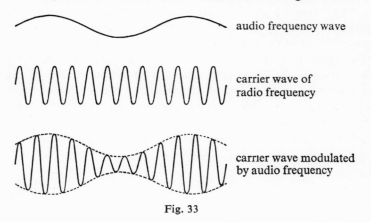

audio frequency wave

carrier wave of radio frequency

carrier wave modulated by audio frequency

Fig. 33

Amplitude modulation is the commonest principle used in radio transmission; however, a more recent technique called *frequency modulation* is also used when especially high fidelity is required. In this method the frequency and not the amplitude of the carrier-wave is modulated by the audio frequency, so that the modulated carrier would have the shape shown in Figure 34.

In order to complete our outline of radio broadcasting it will now be necessary to describe briefly the method of creating carrier-waves in the transmitter, and the method of *demodulating* the carrier in the receiver so that an audio-frequency current can be amplified and fed into the loudspeaker.

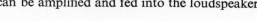

Fig. 34

Transmitters

Firstly, then, we must refer to the production of high-frequency oscillations suitable for use as a carrier-wave.

In our discussion, so far, the only sources of oscillation for the production of electromagnetic waves have been mechanical – a rotating switch, a rotating coil in a magnetic field, and a moving diaphragm operated by the pressure-waves of sound. Now that we come to higher frequencies such mechanical devices are unsuitable because of the inertia associated with matter of relatively large mass. Instead, the oscillations must be produced by making the current of electrons itself self-oscillating. This is achieved by using a resonant circuit, the operation of which will now be outlined.

The Resonant Circuit

A *resonant circuit* consists of an induction coil, such as that in Figure 24, connected to an electrical condenser. A condenser consists simply of two metal plates separated by a non-conductor of electricity, such as mica; this device is capable of storing electrical charges by virtue of the electrons that collect on one of its plates when it is charged. If the condenser is connected to an electric cell it will become charged (Figure 35a), and if the cell is subsequently replaced by an induction coil (Figure 35b), the condenser will discharge itself through the induction coil, thus creating a magnetic field round the coil.

6

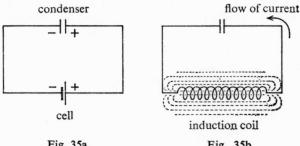

condenser

flow of current

cell

induction coil

Fig. 35a   Fig. 35b

As soon as the condenser is completely discharged the current will cease to flow and the magnetic field will collapse. As we have seen, a changing magnetic field always creates a current, and therefore a secondary current will be induced in the coil in the opposite direction to the main current. This secondary, or self-induced current, will now charge up the condenser in an opposite manner to the original charge (Figure 35c), and again the condenser will discharge itself through the coil, so that a continuous oscillation will be set up in the circuit. The frequency of this oscillation will depend on the capacity of the condenser to store electricity and the ability of the coil to create a magnetic field.

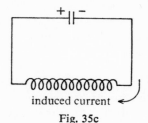

induced current

Fig. 35c

It will be observed that the circuit we have described is in some respects similar to a pendulum swinging backwards and forwards, and, like a pendulum, it will eventually come to rest as the result of friction unless some means is used to supply it with energy to overcome this friction. In the case of a clock, the energy is supplied to the pendulum by a spring or a falling weight through a catchment. Similarly, the resonant circuit cannot oscillate indefinitely as energy has to be consumed in overcoming the resistance to the flow of current through the wire – that is to say energy has to be supplied to drive the electrons back and forth through the wire of the coil. Clearly a device is required which will supply this energy at precisely the right moment, just as the catchment supplies energy to the pendulum at precisely the right moment.

This energy can be supplied to a resonant circuit by using an electronic valve of the type that we have already described, in the following manner. If the oscillating current of a resonant circuit is fed into the grid of a triode valve, an identical but stronger oscillation will be produced in the anode circuit of the valve. If this oscillating anode current is used to reinforce the original oscillation in the resonant circuit the whole device will oscillate indefinitely, as energy is being fed into the system from the batteries operating the valve.

An elementary radio carrier-wave transmitter is illustrated in Figure 36, the conventional symbols being used for the components in the circuit. In the particular type of circuit illustrated, it will be noticed that the oscillation in the resonant circuit is reinforced from the anode circuit by means of a second induction coil, and that the final electromagnetic wave can be transmitted into the atmosphere from an aerial in the anode circuit.

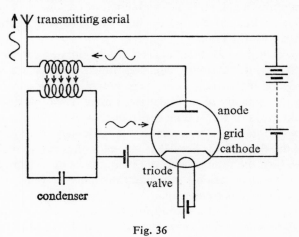

Fig. 36

An arrangement of this type, of course, only produces the carrier-wave; additional circuits are required for carrying out the modulation by an audio-frequency, but we are not here concerned with the details of transmitter design.

Receivers

We must now consider the methods used in a radio receiver for demodulating the electromagnetic radiations sent out by the transmitter so that they will operate a loudspeaker.

Broadly speaking a radio receiver has two main functions to perform; firstly, it has to select the required radiation from all the other electromagnetic waves that are present over the surface of the earth, and secondly it has to separate (or demodulate) the audio-frequency current from the radio-frequency carrier.

The selection is effected by making use of a resonant circuit of the type already described. If a resonant circuit in the receiver is tuned so that it will oscillate at the same frequency as the carrier-wave which is to be received, clearly, of all the electromagnetic waves picked up by the receiving aerial, the only one to be selectively strengthened will be the one with a frequency exactly fitting the resonance of the tuned circuit. We are familiar with this aspect of resonance in connexion with sound-waves; if a note is played on a piano, or other musical instrument, in a room which contains a glass tumbler with a natural resonant frequency the same as that of the note, then the glass will vibrate in resonance with the note.

The receiving aerial, then, collects the modulated carrier-wave and feeds it into a circuit which is tuned to resonate at the frequency of the carrier-wave. This tuning can be effected by altering the capacity of a condenser, which, as we have seen, is one of the ways of controlling the frequency at which a resonant circuit will oscillate. For example, the frequency of the carrier-wave of the BBC Home Service is 908 kilocycles per second, and when we turn the tuning-knob of our radio-sets we usually alter the capacity of a variable condenser so that the tuning-circuit will resonate at this frequency.

We have said that the second function of a receiver is that of demodulating the carrier-wave; again, this operation can be per-

formed by using an electronic valve. So far the only use we have
made of valves has been for amplification, but they also serve
another purpose – *rectification* – that is to say they will only permit
current to flow in one direction. Thus, if a modulated carrier-
wave is fed into the grid of a triode valve, and the bias of the
grid is correctly arranged, only current flowing in one direction
will be passed through the valve, and the bottom half, or negative
swing, of the wave will be cut off, as in Figure 37. It will be seen

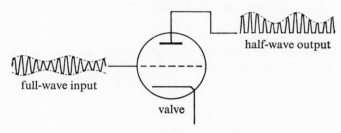

half-wave output

full-wave input

valve

Fig. 37

that the shape traced by the peaks of the emergent half of the
carrier-waves is the same as the original audio-frequency current,
and, if these half-waves are fed into earphones or a loudspeaker,
the original sound wave will be reproduced. The half-waves of
the carrier themselves will not, of course, affect the earphones or
loudspeaker as their frequency is far too high. Demodulation has
therefore been achieved by the use of an electronic valve as a
rectifier.

Rectification can also be brought about by the use of certain
crystals, which have this property of allowing current to pass in
one direction only. These crystals were used in the early days of
radio in crystal sets; transistors are a more modern application of
the same principle.

From what we have said above it is evident that a simple
receiver can be constructed from a resonant circuit and a valve
feeding a pair of earphones as illustrated in Figure 38. More
complicated circuits are of course used in practice, but the
arrangement illustrated would be a quite workable means of
receiving radio signals.

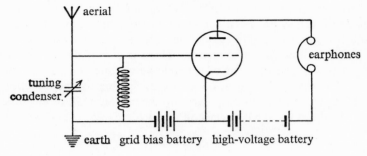

Fig. 38

The general arrangement of simple radio transmission and reception is summarized in Figure 39.

Radar

Electromagnetic waves with a frequency higher than ordinary radio short-waves, that is waves of between about 1 and 10 centimetres in length, are reflected by large solid objects in much the same manner as light. They are, however, able to travel greater distances than light in the earth's atmosphere, because they are not reflected or diffused by small dust particles in the atmosphere. If, therefore, a transmitter sends out a beam of these centimetric waves, an adjacent receiver can be made to pick up any of the beam that is reflected back by a large solid object, and in this way distant objects, which are not visible by light, can be located. By suitable scanning arrangements, the position and shape of the object can be outlined on a cathode-ray tube. Thus, electromagnetic waves of these frequencies, which have come to be called *radar frequencies*, provide a method of 'seeing' in the dark or in fog.

Having now outlined the production and use of electromagnetic energy in the audio- and radio-frequency bands, we may pass to an examination of infra-red frequencies.

HEAT WAVES OR INFRA-RED RADIATION

So far we have been dealing with radiant energy to which the human senses are not directly responsive. (It will be recalled that

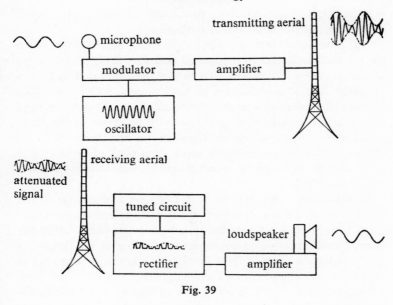

Fig. 39

our ears cannot detect electromagnetic waves of audio frequency, although they respond to pressure waves in the air of these frequencies.) Now, however, that we come to waves of length about one hundredth to one ten-thousandth of a centimetre, we are dealing with *radiant heat* to which the nerves of the skin are sensitive.

In Figure 19 (page 129) it was shown that heat energy is converted into radiant energy by hot body radiation, and it is a common experience that a hot body of matter can cause the nerves of the skin to register the sensation of heat, even when the skin is not in contact with the hot body, and even when the hot body is not radiating visible light. Such radiant heat, or *infra-red radiation*, is transferred by electromagnetic waves within the waveband which we are now considering. These waves have frequencies of from about a million million cycles per second to 100 million, million cycles per second, and such extremely rapid oscillations cannot ordinarily be produced by a current of electrons oscillating backwards and forwards in a circuit. At these very high frequencies the only oscillators with sufficiently small inertia are individual atoms or molecules.

We have seen that an electromagnetic field results when electric charges and their associated magnetic fields are in a state of movement, and we have also seen that the atoms and molecules of matter consist essentially of electric charges. As we know that atoms and molecules are in a continual state of vibration (and rotation, in the case of gases) it is only to be expected that these movements should create electromagnetic radiations. It is an observed fact that vibrations (and rotations) of atomic and molecular particles cause electromagnetic waves in the radiant heat wave-band.

By raising the temperature of a body we add energy to the atoms and molecules of which it consists, and therefore cause them to vibrate more rapidly. The higher the temperature the faster the vibrations and consequently the higher the frequency of the radiation emitted. This increase in frequency continues in the radiant heat-band until a wave-length of about $6 \cdot 5 \times 10^{-5}$ cm. is reached. This is the wave-length of the first *visible* electromagnetic radiation – it is the wave-length of red light; it is for this reason that bodies glow red when their temperatures are raised sufficiently. We shall, however, come to light-waves in the next section; for the present we are considering radiations that are infra- (i.e., less-than) red.

Planck's Constant

In our introductory remarks concerning the nature of energy we referred to its discontinuity and pointed out that, as the quanta of energy are small, they need only be taken into account when dealing with individual atoms or molecules. Now that we have seen that infra-red radiation results from the vibrations of atoms and molecules, we can expect that Quantum Theory considerations must hold in this waveband. This is, in fact, the case, and in order to be able to account for the radiation of heat in a detailed and mathematical way it is essential to think of electromagnetic waves as being emitted in quanta, or short bursts of energy – each quantum being of a definite size.

The size of these energy quanta depends on the frequency of the emitted radiation and can be calculated by simply multiplying the frequency by a universal constant which is known as *Planck's Constant* (after the discoverer). This constant (which is symbolized by the letter h) figures in all the equations of contemporary physics which are in any way connected with the energy of individual atoms. As the value of Planck's constant is very small indeed, i.e., 6.6×10^{-27} erg seconds (an erg is a unit of energy equal to 2.4×10^{-8} calories), the quanta of energy are also very small and therefore, as we have already stated, need not be taken into account when dealing with any large quantity of matter. For atomic particles, however, they have a restrictive effect in that only certain speeds of vibration or rotation are possible – that is, speeds that will give whole numbers of energy quanta, because parts of a quantum cannot exist.

From these quantum considerations we have to accept the difficult conception that electromagnetic waves of energy are not simply analogous to waves in a pond of water, but that they are given out in short bursts. These bursts, as the wave-lengths become shorter, develop properties that we associate with particles. Furthermore, as we shall see later, electrons, which appear as particles, also have certain properties associated with waves. These paradoxes are partly resolved by the theory of wave mechanics, which we shall refer to on page 178.

Having briefly described infra-red radiations and the necessity for thinking in terms of quanta, we can now pass into the range of visible wave-lengths.

LIGHT RADIATION

The most familiar of all electromagnetic radiations are those to which the retina of the eye is sensitive, that is, those which we call *light*. It should provoke humility to reflect that our total visual conception of the universe is formed by those electro-magnetic radiations which are emitted or reflected by matter, within the very narrow waveband of 4.1×10^{-5} cm. to 6.5×10^{-5} cm. A glance at Table 4 (page 151) will show just how narrow this waveband really is.

The Visible Spectrum

To appreciate the meaning of colour in the universe, we must now consider the structure of the *visible spectrum*.

If a ray of white light, from the sun or an electric lamp, is passed through a glass prism (a solid of triangular cross-section), the white light will be split up into a range of different colours, as in Figure 40. These seven colours are the principal colours of the visible spectrum, and each colour corresponds to a definite frequency and wave-length. The wave-length of red light is the longest, being 6.5×10^{-5} cm., and the wave-length of the violet light is the shortest at 4.1×10^{-5} cm. Electromagnetic radiation of shorter wave-length than that of violet light ceases to be visible to the human eye, and such shorter waves belong to the ultra-violet region, which we shall discuss in the next section.

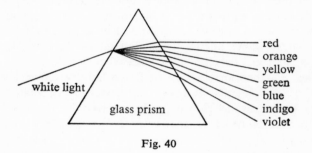

Fig. 40

Although we have illustrated the visible spectrum as seven separate colours, it is important to realize that each colour merges into the next, so that between each one of the seven pure colours there exists a narrow region of blended colours. The visible spectrum of colours is familiar to us in the rainbow, which results from the sun's light being split up into its constituent colours as it passes through rain-drops.

Refraction of Light

From the remarks which we have made it will be apparent that white light is nothing more than a mixture of all the colours of the visible spectrum in certain proportions. In order to discover the reasons for the separation of these components when white light passes from one medium to another (e.g., air to glass, air to water), we have to examine the causes of the *refraction of light*. All electromagnetic radiations travel at exactly the same velocity in empty space, but this velocity is reduced when they pass through matter. The extent of the reduction depends on the nature of the matter and the frequency of the radiation – the higher the frequency the greater the reduction in velocity. If the frequency of a radiation remains unchanged, and the speed of travel is reduced, it will be obvious from the considerations on page 150 that the wave-length will be shortened. The result of this shortening of the wave-length is to cause a bending or refraction of the wave at the interface between two mediums, as illustrated in Figure 41.

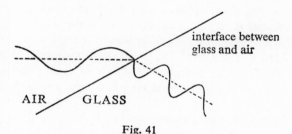

Fig. 41

Clearly, then, when white light enters a prism, the violet component, owing to its higher frequency, will suffer a greater shortening of wave-length than the red component and will therefore be refracted through a greater angle than the red light. The intermediate colours will be refracted through intermediate angles, and the overall result of the refraction of white light will be to separate its components according to their frequencies. A prism has been chosen to illustrate this point because two refractions occur, one at each face, the effect of the second refraction being to amplify the first. We have said that the extent to which a wave of light is refracted depends on the frequency of the wave and also upon the material causing the refraction. Every material behaves in a characteristic manner in this respect, which is defined by its so-called *refractive index*.

Colour

In our description of light so far, we have mentioned only white light and the way in which it is split into its component colours. We have not explained why non-emitters of light can have distinctive colours, and we must now consider this question.

The pages of this book do not emit light, but they reflect the light from the sun, or an artificial source such as an electric lamp. The paper of the page appears to be white, because it is a good reflector and reflects back to the reader's eye all the colours emitted by the source of light which illuminates it. On the other hand, the ink appears black, because it is a bad reflector and it absorbs all the light that falls upon it so that no light is reflected from its surface to the eye of the reader. Lipstick, for example, is red because it absorbs all the white light that falls upon it except the red component, which it reflects. Similarly, grass is green because it reflects only the green component of the sun's light. Furthermore, if a tube of lipstick is taken into a darkroom, where there is only a red light, it will still appear red, because red light is available for reflection. A blade of grass, however, will appear black, because there is no green light available for it to reflect.

Thus, the colour of a non-emitter of light is purely a question of the colours which it absorbs and the colours which it reflects. We shall learn later about the factors which control whether a particular atom or molecule will absorb or reflect a radiation of a particular frequency (or colour).

The Emission of Light

In the last section it was shown that electromagnetic radiation of infra-red frequencies was produced as a result of the vibrations and rotations of atoms and molecules. However, even atoms are too heavy to oscillate at the frequencies corresponding to light, and we now have to consider the movements of the orbital electrons of the individual atoms.

It might be thought that the high-speed rotation of an electron in its orbit round the nucleus of an atom could, in itself, constitute a source of electromagnetic radiation of frequency equal to the speed of rotation. Such a supposition would be in accord with everything we have said so far about the movement of electric charges and electromagnetic fields. It does, however, illustrate the danger of trying to use common-sense reasoning within the atom. As we shall see, when we come to examine the nucleus in more detail, the laws which apply to electric charges outside the atom do not appear to be obeyed within the nucleus.

The apparently reasonable explanation which we have suggested for the emission of light by orbital electrons of atoms can be shown to be incorrect by means of a simple experiment. If pure hydrogen gas is heated sufficiently it will emit light, and if this light is passed through a prism it will be found that narrow and distinct lines occur in place of the continuous visible spectrum derived from white light. Of these lines two predominate as the most persistent, one red and the other green.

Clearly, then, hydrogen is only capable of emitting radiation at certain distinct frequencies. On the other hand, if the rotation of the electron was the source, one would expect a continuous range of colours to be emitted, because the emission of energy by the electron (and there is only one in the hydrogen atom) would cause it to slow down gradually and thus produce radiation of ever-decreasing frequency. The fact that the visible spectrum of hydrogen consists of separate lines indicates that some other mechanism must be sought to account for radiations of optical frequencies. As we shall see later, in the final answer it is necessary to reconsider the idea of an electron as a particle, but before abandoning this helpful conception altogether we can make use of it once more.

The Bohr Atom

In our analysis of matter we described the electrons surrounding the nucleus of an atom as arranging themselves into 'shells' (see page 30). In order to visualize the manner in which energy is stored by these electrons, we must now depict them as being capable of existence at different energy-levels within the shell – the higher the energy-level the greater the distance of the orbit from the nucleus.

To complete the picture, we have to assume that such orbital electrons are only capable of emitting or absorbing energy when they jump from one energy-level to another, and at no other time. This is in accord with the Quantum Theory, which as we have seen postulates that energy is emitted, on the atomic scale, in short bursts. When an electron jumps inwards towards the nucleus, it loses energy which is emitted as a quantum of light, called a *photon*. Conversely, if a quantum of energy is absorbed by the atom (and this can only happen if it is exactly the right size), then the electron jumps outwards from the nucleus, still remaining within the correct shell. In the case of the hydrogen atom, then, we can imagine three such energy-levels or possible orbits for the sole electron (Figure 42) to account for the two

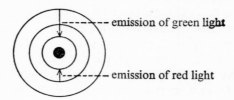

emission of green light

emission of red light

Fig. 42

predominant visible emissions which we have mentioned. In fact, of course, the position is very much more complicated than this as we have only taken into account the most predominant of the visible emission lines.

This picture of possible orbits corresponding to energy-levels is called the *Bohr atom*, after its initiator, and it provides in many respects an adequate working model, being particularly well suited to the depiction of the emission of energy in quanta. It should be noted that Bohr's Theory has been amplified mathematically to take into account the fact that electron orbits can be elliptical and that the electrons themselves are capable of spinning on their own axis.

However, the Bohr atom, even in its modified form, still relies on the electron as a particle, and for reasons which we shall now outline, it cannot be accepted as an actual representation of fact. It is not correct to assume that if a sufficiently powerful microscope were available we should be able to watch electrons jumping from one orbit to another. The main reason for this assertion is that the actual act of observation would alter the process being observed, as we shall see from the following considerations.

The Uncertainty Principle

It has been proved that the energy of a light quantum, or photon, which would be required to 'illuminate' an electron, so that it could be observed, would alter the position of the electron. The electron and the photon may be visualized in this sense as two colliding billiard balls – after collision both balls alter their course to an extent which depends on the energy of motion contained by each of them before collision.

This is the basis of the *Heisenberg Uncertainty Principle*, which states that the position and the velocity of an electron cannot both be known exactly – the magnitude of the error, if both these measurements were to be made simultaneously, would be very great, but it can be calculated. This dilemma is not an experimental difficulty; it is fundamental and cannot be resolved. The position and velocity of the ultimate particles of nature cannot be defined without uncertainty.

This being the case, it is perhaps illogical to expect that we should be able to visualize accurately something that nature precludes us from seeing accurately. Therefore the Bohr atom may be accepted as a useful method of understanding some aspects of the subject, but it must not be regarded as a true description of the inner workings of an atom.

Interference

In order to gain a more fundamental understanding of the behaviour of electrons within the atom, it is necessary to examine the way in which they behave as waves, as opposed to particles. In order to do so, reference must be made to the phenomenon of *interference* which is exhibited by light-waves.

If a ray of light from a source is allowed to fall on a sheet of paper in which a small slit has been made (A in Figure 43), and if the beam of light which emerges from this slit is allowed to fall upon a second sheet of paper which contains two small holes (B and C) so that A is equidistant from B and C, then the waves of

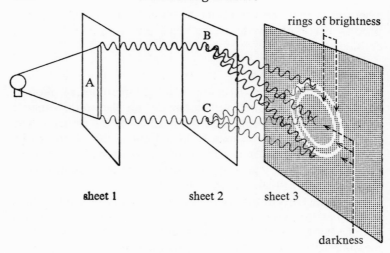

Fig. 43

light arriving at B and C will be exactly in phase (that is to say that the crests of the waves will arrive at B and C at the same instant).

Now, if the beams which emerge from the holes B and C are allowed to fall on a third sheet of paper, a characteristic pattern will be observed on this third sheet which typifies all wave motion. Where the two circles of light falling on the third sheet of paper overlap there will be alternate concentric rings of darkness and brightness which are called *interference rings*. The dark circles occur where the waves of light from the two holes B and C arrive on sheet 3 out of phase with each other, thus cancelling each other out, as in Figure 44. This cancelling effect of two

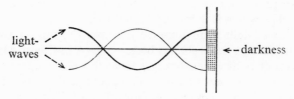

Fig. 44

waves out of phase with each other can be visualized by thinking of a cork floating on a pool of water. A wave coming from one direction will lift the cork to the height of its crest as it passes. If, however, a wave of equal amplitude comes from the opposite direction so that its trough arrives at the cork at exactly the same instant as the crest of the first wave, the cork will remain stationary as the effect of the two waves cancel each other out. In exactly the same way, two light-waves arriving at a point will, if they are out of phase, result in darkness. Similarly the bright circles in the interference patterns occur where the waves arrive in phase with each other, and so their effect is doubled.

These interference experiments prove conclusively that light is associated with a wave-motion, for if it consisted only of particles (photons), it would be impossible to explain how two particles arriving at the same point could cancel each other out – they could only reinforce each other, and interference patterns would not occur. On the other hand, however, when we come to examine the photo-electric effect, it will become evident that light has properties that can only be explained in terms of particles. Thus light (and the other short-wave electromagnetic radiations) present us with the same duality as electrons. Both are associated partly with waves of energy (emitted in short bursts according to the Quantum Theory) and partly with particles. We shall refer to the resolution of this paradox when we say something about wave mechanics.

As far as electrons are concerned, it has been shown experimentally that they behave in exactly the same manner as light with regard to interference, and it must therefore be concluded that a beam of electrons possesses at least one characteristic of a wave-motion. That electrons do in fact possess wave properties is now well established, and it has been found that the length of the associated wave is dependent upon the velocity with which the electron is moving – the faster it moves, the shorter its associated wave-length. To be precise, the actual wave-length (λ) is obtained by dividing Planck's constant (h) by the product of the mass (m) and the velocity of the electron (v), i.e.:

$$\lambda = \frac{h}{mv}$$

Wave Mechanics

The fact that electrons exhibit the properties of both waves and particles has led to the development of a method of expressing this behaviour mathematically which is called *wave mechanics*. Being highly mathematical this treatment does not easily lend itself to descriptive presentation. However, it is possible to interpret the wave-mechanics equations for an electron as expressing the probability that an electron, visualized as a particle, will exist at a certain point in the path of a wave.

The word 'probability' is most important in this context, because according to wave mechanics all the fundamental processes of nature are controlled by probabilities, rather than rigid and inflexible laws. Nothing in the universe is absolutely certain to happen: if it is very likely it has a high probability, if it is very unlikely it has a low probability.

Referred to electrons within the atom, this treatment yields an atomic nucleus, surrounded by a 'cloud of probability' that electrons will exist at certain positions at certain instants of time. These probable positions replace the unnaturally precise positions depicted in the Bohr atom. The greater lack of precision inherent in the wave-mechanical interpretation is accounted for by the Heisenberg Uncertainty Principie.

The dual nature of light is similarly explained by wave mechanics – photons and waves are related by probabilities much in the same way as electrons and waves.

The Electron Microscope

It is worth noting in passing that the wave characteristics of a beam of electrons have been put to a most beneficial use in the electron microscope. Until the invention of this instrument, just before the Second World War, the magnification obtainable with a microscope was limited by the wavelength of visible light. This is because two points on a microscopic specimen cannot be distinguished from each other if they are not at least as far apart as half the wave-length of the light used to illuminate them.

By using a beam of electrons instead of light as the illuminant, virtually any wave-length can be used by controlling the velocity of the electrons electrically. (The wave-length of a beam of electrons, it will be remembered, is inversely proportional to their velocity – that is, the greater the velocity, the shorter the associated wave-length.) Thus, by subjecting a beam of electrons to a potential of 10,000 volts a wave-length of about 10^{-9} cm. is obtained, compared to visible wave-lengths of the order of 5×10^{-5} cm. Glass lenses cannot be used with electron microscopes; instead a system of magnetic lenses has been developed, and the resulting image is photographed on a special type of photographic plate. With the tremendous magnifications possible with this instrument, objects as small as individual viruses can now be clearly photographed and observed.

Emission Spectra

From the foregoing paragraphs we are led to conclude that, although the positions of the orbital electrons as particles cannot be precisely defined, they can be visualized as existing at certain points in the path of a wave, and, while they do not emit radiation continuously, they do so when they jump from a high energy level to a lower one.

When these jumps take place a photon of light energy is emitted; the size of the photon, and therefore the frequency of the associated wave, depends upon the magnitude of the jump and hence upon the 'probable' arrangement of the electrons within the atom. As the atoms of the different chemical elements contain different numbers and groupings of electrons, it is not surprising that the frequencies at which light is emitted differ from one element to another.

We have seen that the emission of light from incandescent hydrogen when passed through a prism produces a series of lines in place of the continuous visible spectrum. The arrangement of these lines is called the *emission line spectrum* of hydrogen. All the other elements, when heated to incandescence in the gaseous state, also produce characteristic emission line spectra, and as the position and strength of these lines differ from element to element, any element can be identified by its emission line spectrum. For example, sodium vapour produces a very strong and persistent line of wave-length 5.9×10^{-5} cm.;* as this is the frequency of yellow light, the addition of common salt (sodium chloride) to a flame will colour it bright yellow. Similarly, strontium has a strong line in the red region of the visible spectrum and will colour a flame bright red.

Gas molecules also produce characteristic spectral lines, but, owing to the complications resulting from the presence of two or more atoms in the molecule, the lines are much more closely packed together and are known as *band spectra*.

Visual line and band spectra are only produced by atoms and molecules in the gaseous state, because in the liquid or solid states the atoms and molecules are so near to each other that the individual radiations are interfered with and superimposed upon one another so that a continuous spectrum is produced.

This principle can be illustrated by supplying heat energy to a solid piece of metal (or any other material which does not vaporize at too low a temperature). Up to a temperature of about 550°C the radiation will all be in the infra-red, and hence the metal will not alter its appearance although it will be radiating heat. Above 550°C, the metal will begin to glow with a red light (red heat) which will become lighter and lighter as the temperature is raised, until about 1,300°C is reached. At this temperature the metal will glow with white light (white heat), because all the colours of the visible spectrum are being emitted in approximately the correct proportions for white light. This, of course, is how white light is obtained from electric-light bulbs – a metal filament is heated to white heat by an electric current. At still higher temperatures the metal would take on a bluish tinge owing to the predominance of the high-frequency violet light, although most metals vaporize at the temperature corresponding to blue light (and as vapours they emit line spectra).

In these examples we have illustrated the emission of light as a result of energy being supplied to matter in the form of heat, but it must also be mentioned that gases can be provoked to emit radiant energy by bombarding the atoms and molecules of which they consist with a stream of electrons. For example, a neon-tube

---

* Sodium actually produces two lines, so close together that a simple instrument shows them as one.

light is simply a tube of glass filled with the inert gas neon, through which a current of electrons is caused to flow. If the voltage is correctly adjusted to give the electrons the required amount of energy to knock the orbital electrons of the neon atoms into a lower energy level, the tube will emit its characteristic red light.

Absorption Spectra

If white light is passed through a pure gas, and then through a prism, it will be found that the continuous spectrum normally produced by white light is interrupted by dark lines at exactly the positions occupied by the coloured lines of the emission spectrum of that gas. For example, if the gas consists of sodium vapour, the continuous spectrum will have, amongst others, a black line in the yellow region corresponding to a wave-length of 5.9×10^{-5} cm. Such dark lines are called *absorption line spectra*, and are due to the selective absorption, by the atoms of the gas, of radiations of the same frequency as they are capable of emitting. The fact that a gas can only absorb energy at those frequencies which it is capable of emitting is analogous to the phenomenon of resonance which we have mentioned in connexion with sound-waves and electrical circuits.

The atoms and molecules of a solid, however, are too tightly packed to be able to be selective about the frequencies at which they will resonate, just as they are unable to be selective about the frequencies which they emit. Solids, therefore, absorb light of most frequencies, which accounts for the fact that they are usually opaque. Some solids, on the other hand, are transparent because they are without the ability of resonating in the visible range of frequencies, and they are therefore incapable of absorbing light. As we have seen earlier, the colour of an opaque solid or liquid is determined by the wave-lengths it is incapable of absorbing, that is, by the wave-lengths it reflects.

Absorption spectra present us with a method of discovering which of the elements exist in the sun and the stars. The interior of the sun, it will be recalled, is a glowing mass of matter radiating white light which must pass through the surface and atmosphere of the sun before reaching the earth. Thus, if sunlight is passed through a prism, dark lines will appear in the continuous spectrum so obtained, and from the position and strength of these lines it is possible to tell which of the elements are present on the surface and in the atmosphere of the sun. This method can also be applied to light from the stars, and from the results obtained it has been possible to conclude that the rest of the visible universe is composed of the same ninety-two elements with which we are familiar on earth. The method of analysing emission and absorption spectra is known as *spectroscopy*, and the instrument used, containing the prism or other suitable device, is called a *spectroscope*.

The Red Shift

In addition to giving information concerning the constitution of the stars, spectroscopy can also provide certain information concerning their motions.

The movement of a star through space, relative to the earth, can be observed through a telescope provided that the star is not moving either directly towards, or away from, the earth. Clearly, taking into account the enormous distances concerned, looking at a star through a telescope will not disclose if it is moving directly towards or away from the earth, nor will it disclose any component which the star's movement may have in these directions. This information can, however, be obtained from the star's spectrum in the following manner.

Consider a star which is emitting light of a particular frequency – say yellow light. We know that the colour of light is determined by its frequency, that is, in this case, by the number of waves per second arriving in the spectroscope. Now, if the spectroscope is travelling towards the star, or the star towards the spectroscope, the number of waves per second which arrive will obviously be increased; consequently the apparent frequency of the light will be increased and the colour of the light will be shifted towards the violet (high frequency) end of the spectrum. Conversely, if the star is receding from the earth, the colour of the visible radiation which it emits will be shifted towards the red end of the spectrum. By measuring the extent of these shifts, the velocity of the star, towards or away from the earth, can be calculated.

It is evidence of this *red shift* that has led astronomers to conclude that the universe is expanding, that is, that its components are flying apart. (See page 224.)

The Photo-electric Effect

We have shown that, as a result of the interference effect, light must have wave properties; we have also mentioned that these waves are emitted in quanta, or bursts of energy, called photons which can in some contexts be regarded as particles.

Just as electrons appear to be particles with certain wave properties, so light appears to be a wave with some particle properties. That the ultimate components of matter (electrons) and the ultimate components of energy (photons) should have similar dual natures is not surprising bearing in mind the close relationship which exists between matter and energy. We shall say more about this later; for the present we must refer to the corpuscular (particle-like) properties exhibited by photons in the *photo-electric effect*.

If a ray of light is allowed to fall on a clean metal surface (in a vacuum for the best results) the energy of the light will be absorbed by the free electrons in the metal, some of which will thereby acquire sufficient energy to escape from the surface of the metal. It has been found that the number of electrons to escape depends upon the strength of the light – that is upon the *number* of photons; but the speed of the escaping electrons (i.e., their energy) depends upon the *size* of the photons, that is upon the frequency of the incident light. (It will be remembered that the size of a photon is equal to the frequency of the radiation it embodies multiplied by Planck's constant.)

Thus a very weak source of violet light will cause the emission of faster electrons by the photo-electric effect than will a very strong source of red light. Purely on a wave basis this state of affairs would be incomprehensible; it can only be explained if the light is visualized as being composed of particles the size of which is a measure of the energy they contain in accordance with the Quantum Theory. In fact, owing to its low frequency, red light consists of photons which are insufficiently energetic to cause a photo-electric effect with most metals, but violet light frees electrons from nearly all metals. Ultra-violet and X-radiations produce very fast electrons because their photons contain more energy than visible light.

The photo-electric effect is made use of very widely in the photo-electric cell. This is somewhat similar to the electronic valve which we have already described (see page 158), but, in the photo-cell the cathode is provoked into electron emission by illumination, not by heating. The electrons so produced travel directly to the anode without the intermediary of a grid, and create a current which will fluctuate in accordance with the strength of the illumination falling upon the cathode.

This principle is often used in the production of sound in cinematograph projectors. Light from a powerful lamp is passed through the sound-track on the film, and the fluctuating illumination produced by the shadows of the sound-track is allowed to fall on a photocell, the output of which is fed into an amplifier and loudspeakers. In this way the shadows on the sound-track are converted into sound.

ULTRA-VIOLET RADIATION

In discussing the emission of electromagnetic radiation by atoms, we have so far only mentioned those that have too low a frequency to be visible (i.e., infra-red radiations) and those that are visible (i.e., light). However, atoms also emit radiations that have too great a frequency to be visible; these are called, in order of increasing frequency, *ultra-violet radiation*, *X-radiation*, and *γ-radiation*. In this section we shall deal with ultra-violet radiation and in the subsequent section we shall say something about X-and γ-radiations.

Ultra-violet radiations, then, are electromagnetic radiations which have wave-lengths between 4×10^{-5} cm. and 3×10^{-6} cm., and which are emitted by atoms in the same way as light. In general their properties are very similar to those of light, with the notable exception that the retina of the human eye is not sensitive to them.

All the elements of the Periodic Table produce their own characteristic spectral lines in the ultra-violet frequency range, just as they produce characteristic lines in the visible waveband,

and these lines can be recorded, by a spectroscope, on a photographic plate. For although ultra-violet radiations cannot be seen, they can be recorded photographically as they have the same effect on a photographic emulsion as light.

The emissions from the sun include ultra-violet radiations of most wave-lengths as well as the visible frequencies, although some of the shorter wave-lengths are strongly absorbed by the earth's atmosphere and therefore do not reach us on the earth's surface. In fact, the shorter the wave-length of ultra-violet radiations, the greater their absorption by the atmosphere, until a wave-length of about 3×10^{-6} cm. is reached when the penetrating power of the radiations begins to increase. However, radiations of shorter wave-length than this are the subject of the next section, as they are called X-rays.

The ultra-violet component of sunlight is of interest to us for three principal reasons: firstly, it causes sun tan; secondly, it ionizes the upper atmosphere so that the reflection of sky waves in radio broadcasting can be achieved; and thirdly, certain reactions can only take place in the presence of ultra-violet radiation – one such reaction leads to the formation of vitamin D without which young mammals (including children) develop rickets.

The sun tan is produced by ultra-violet radiation of a narrow band of wave-lengths around 3×10^{-5} cm. but, as radiations in this waveband are absorbed by the atmosphere to a certain extent, winter sunshine at sea-level causes hardly any tan as the sun's rays have to pass through a greater thickness of atmosphere than they do in the summer. At sea-level in the summer or on high mountains in the winter the thickness of atmosphere is not sufficient to absorb all the ultra-violet radiations of this frequency and therefore sun tan results. We have already mentioned the useful effect that ultra-violet radiations cause in the ionosphere (p. 159), and we shall have more to say on ionization caused by electromagnetic radiations in the next section.

X-RADIATION AND γ-RADIATION

X-rays and γ-rays have very similar properties: in fact, γ-rays are only X-rays of particularly short wave-length and penetrating power. The distinction between these two radiations concerns their origin and generation rather than their properties, for, while X-rays are emitted by the inner orbital electrons of atoms, γ-rays are emitted by their nuclei. In Chapter 2 we said that γ-rays are emitted by the naturally radioactive atoms when they break down, with the emanation of α- or β-particles: we shall discuss this aspect of nuclear physics in greater detail in Chapter 11; for the present we must say something more about the emission of X-rays.

The Emission of X-rays

In the previous sections we have shown how visible and ultra-violet radiations are produced when *outer* electrons of an atom jump from one energy-level to a lower one. However, X-rays being of wave-lengths 3×10^{-6} cm. to 3×10^{-9} cm. are very considerably more energetic than optical radiations, and are therefore concerned with the *inner* orbital electrons. This is because the inner electrons, particularly of the heavier elements, are held in their orbits round the nucleus with greater binding energy than the outer electrons; it is therefore to be expected that, when these inner electrons jump from one energy-level to a lower one, the quanta emitted will be of greater energy than those emitted by the outer electrons. Indeed, the X-ray spectra emitted by the various atoms of the elements have yielded a considerable amount of information concerning the arrangement and con-figuration of the inner electrons of atoms.

The fact that X-rays are associated with energy levels of the inner electrons accounts for the fact that atoms produce spectral lines in the X-ray waveband even when they are combined in molecules, or are in the solid state. As chemical combination and physical state depends on the behaviour of the outer electrons, inner electrons and the X-radiations which they emit are un-influenced by such matters. The inner electrons of an atom are provoked into X-ray emission by bombarding the atom with a beam of fast-moving electrons; the faster the electrons in the beam, the deeper into the atom they penetrate and therefore the higher the frequency of the emitted X-rays.

A typical source of X-rays for medical purposes consists of an evacuated glass tube containing a hot wire filament which produces the beam of electrons (F in Figure 45). These electrons bombard a small disk of a heavy metal such as platinum (D in the figure), the atoms of which contain inner electrons bound to the nucleus with high energy. A very high voltage is applied to this disk, which forms part of a massive copper anode (A), and the heated filament (F) is suspended in a specially shaped cathode which produces a narrow beam of electrons. The general arrangement is similar to that of the electronic valve which has already been described, but, in this case, the effect of a high-energy stream of electrons on the atoms of platinum is to disorganize their inner electrons so that they fall to a lower energy-level, giving off photons of X-radiation in the process.

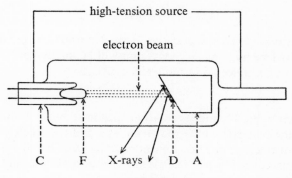

Fig. 45

Owing to their high penetrating power, these X-rays will pass through matter as long as it is not too dense; the use of X-rays for medical diagnosis depends on the fact that they are more strongly absorbed by bone than by flesh. Thus, if an X-ray tube is placed above a limb and a photographic plate is placed beneath it, a shadow of the bone will be formed on the plate. This procedure can be used to discover whether a bone is fractured or not. In a similar manner X-rays can be used to examine the outline of a stomach, or other internal organ, by giving the patient a dose of a liquid (such as a 'barium meal') which is opaque to X-rays (i.e., a liquid which absorbs X-rays).

Ionizing Radiation

We must now say something about the ionization produced by X- and γ-radiations.

In the section on the photo-electric effect it was stated that a stream of photons of the comparatively low energy associated with visible light could liberate from the surface of a metal its loosely bonded free electrons. Photons of X- and γ-rays (and to a lesser extent ultra-violet rays) can, on account of their higher energy, knock outer electrons of an atom from their orbits thus creating positively charged ions (see page 34). For this reason X- and γ-radiations (and high-frequency ultra-violet radiations) are known as *ionizing radiations*. For example, if a water molecule is subjected to X-radiation it will ionize thus:

$$H_2O \xrightarrow{\text{X-ray}} H_2O^+ + e^-$$

The liberated electron will cause further ionizations, but it will eventually lose most of its energy and will be finally collected by another water molecule forming a negative ion:

$$e^- + H_2O \rightarrow H_2O^-$$

In general, then, X- and γ-radiations produce free electrons and ions in the material which they irradiate, and the free electrons will in turn cause further ionizations. In fact, the number of ionizations caused by the free electrons is several thousand times greater than the number of ionizations resulting from the X- and γ-radiations themselves.

The chemical effect of ionizing radiations is due to the exceptional reactivity of the ions which, as we have seen, are formed to a large extent by the electrons liberated by the radiation. It is therefore to be expected that β-rays, which consist of a stream of electrons, would also behave as an ionizing radiation, and such is, in fact, the case. But X- and γ-radiations are much more penetrating, energy for energy, than β-rays, and therefore they produce ionization much deeper into the body of the material irradiated by them than β-rays.

In passing it should be noted that some photons will only have sufficient energy (for example light and ultra-violet rays) to raise the energy level of an orbital electron without being able to detach it from the nucleus. Atoms or molecules containing these high-energy electrons are said to be 'excited', and like ions they are exceptionally reactive chemically. This accounts for the fact that some reactions will only take place in the presence of light or ultra-violet radiation.

Because of the high degree of chemical reactivity which they produce, ionizing radiations are extremely dangerous to living organisms, interfering with the functioning of their cells in a manner which is not yet fully understood. Cells can be affected in three ways:

1. They can be disorganized so that their function is upset.
2. They can be disorganized so that their reproductive mechanism is disturbed (mutations, etc.).
3. They can be disorganized to such an extent that they are killed.

In this connexion, it is well known that X- and γ-rays can either cause or cure cancer, depending on the way in which they are administered. They cause cancer by destroying or interfering with some part of the reproductive mechanism of cells so that they proliferate in an uncontrolled manner. They can also be used to cure cancer by killing the malignant cells which are often more susceptible to ionizing radiations than are the healthy cells of the surrounding tissue. Ionizing radiations can also cure cancer by putting the reproductive mechanism of the malignant cells out of action; in such cases the malignant growth does not disappear for some time, although it will have been rendered harmless.

A particular danger of ionizing radiation to life, in even relatively small doses, is that it can cause mutation of genes (see Chapter 6), and in such cases it is not the irradiated organism which suffers but its progeny. It must be remembered, however, that the whole course of evolution has depended upon such mutations (partly as a result of natural background radiation), although in the case of highly developed creatures such as man they are now almost always degenerative. As the effect of ionizing radiation in this respect may be cumulative, the greatest possible care has to be taken in their use for diagnostic and other purposes. In recent years, since these properties of ionizing radiations have been better understood, the use of X-ray machines, in shoe-shops for example, has been discouraged.

The greatest potentially dangerous source of ionizing radiations is nuclear weapons. As we shall see in Chapter 11 the explosion of a nuclear bomb is accompanied by a prolific emanation of γ-rays, which constitute an additional hazard to the heat radiation and the blast (shock-waves) associated with other explosives. The effect on human beings of exposure to γ-radiations from nuclear explosions depends on their distance from the explosion. If they are close enough they will be killed as a result of the death of a sufficient number of cells in vital organs (that is if the heat or the blast has not already killed them). Those who survive are very liable to develop malignant diseases, while those who think they have escaped may have, in fact, suffered genetic damage which may appear as malformation or deficiency of one kind or another in their offspring.

It is not possible, therefore, to exaggerate the appalling consequences that a nuclear war would involve, nor should the people of the world be allowed to forget that each nuclear bomb that is tested adds to the background of ionizing radiation and may well be the cause of at least some deleterious change to human genetic material somewhere.

It must be added that, while X- and γ-radiations are potentially extremely dangerous to mankind, they are also of great value in medicine, both diagnostically and therapeutically. It is to be hoped, therefore, that scientists all over the world will be encouraged to devote their energies exclusively to the development of their beneficial uses.

COSMIC RADIATION

At about the beginning of this century it was found that air, sealed in a closed vessel, was ionized to a small extent, and that the degree of ionization could be reduced by screening the vessel with lead sheeting. It was therefore concluded that the cause of the ionization was coming from outside the vessel, and it was assumed that the ionizing radiation responsible emanated from the small quantity of natural radioactive elements that are found in the earth's crust.

This assumption, however, proved to be only part of the answer, for it was later found, as a result of experiments with high-altitude balloons, that the intensity of the ionizing radiation fell off as the height above the surface of the earth increased, but that after a certain distance had been travelled it began steadily to increase again. It was therefore clear that some ionizing radiations were coming into the earth's atmosphere from outer space, and for this reason they were called *cosmic rays*.

The origin of these rays is still not known, but it appears likely that at least a small portion emanate from the sun, as solar disturbances are accompanied by a small increase in cosmic radiation. On the other hand it is equally clear that the bulk of the radiation does not come from the sun, as it is almost as strong at night as it is in the day. In fact it is now accepted that most of the cosmic radiation arriving on the earth comes from outside the Solar System, and that the primary radiation, that is the radiation as it arrives from space before it has interacted with the atoms of the earth's atmosphere, consists of atomic nuclei, most of which are protons but some of which are heavier particles.

The energy of these particles when they arrive in the earth's atmosphere is extremely great, and therefore the frequencies associated with them are correspondingly high – some being as high as about 10^{24} cycles per second, far higher than even γ-rays. In view of this enormous energy it is not surprising to discover that cosmic radiations interact with the atoms of the atmosphere, and that some of the interactions are with the nuclei of the atoms. Indeed, cosmic rays have been extremely useful to scientists as these interactions have been responsible for most of our knowledge of the structure and components of the atomic nucleus, several new subatomic particles having been discovered as a result of cosmic-ray research.

Positive electrons, called *positrons*, were discovered in this way. These positrons have the same mass as the electron and their charge, though equal in magnitude, is opposite in sense (i.e., they are positively charged). Positrons are formed together with electrons as a result of the materialization of energy during the following sequence of transformations.

If a primary cosmic proton collides with an orbital electron of an atmospheric atom, it will impart to it a great part of its enormous energy. As a result of this acquisition of energy the electron will travel at a velocity very close to the velocity of light, and consequently will have the ability of passing right through the orbital electrons of other atmospheric atoms, so that in some cases such an electron will strike a nucleus. When this happens a photon of extremely high-energy γ-radiation will be produced which can, in certain circumstances, materialize into an electron pair (one electron and one positron): $\gamma \rightarrow e^- + e^+$.

This is an example of the direct creation of matter from energy. However, we have an example of the reverse process when the positron so formed collides with another electron – for then both particles disappear in a photon of γ-radiation, but this will be a less energetic photon, of course, than the photon from which the electron pair was formed. Further subatomic particles called *mesons* have also been discovered as a result of cosmic-ray investigations, but these particles will be discussed in greater detail in Chapter 11.

It should be added that although cosmic rays are very highly energetic, as atomic figures go, they do not arrive on the earth in very great numbers – only a few thousand arrive on an area of the atmosphere the size of this page in one hour. A further point is that, despite the fact that many of the cosmic particles are subject to interactions with the atoms of the atmosphere, some manage to penetrate through to the earth's surface where they add to the natural background of ionizing radiation.

Radio-carbon Dating

An interesting consequence of cosmic radiation is the recently devised method of dating ancient specimens of wood and other organic materials that archaeologists have dug out of the remains of past civilizations.

The impact of cosmic particles on the nitrogen atoms of the atmosphere causes some of them to transform into radioactive carbon atoms of atomic weight 14. We shall say more about these artificial radioactive isotopes in Chapter 11, but here we may say that this particular reaction is provoked by the impact on a nitrogen atom of a neutron (either a primary cosmic particle or the result of a collision between a primary particle and another atom).

The neutron (written n_0^1) becomes embedded in the nitrogen atom (N_7^{14}) which as a result is unstable and ejects a proton (H_1^1), thus forming a nucleus which contains only six protons – this is therefore a carbon nucleus (C_6^{14}) with an unusually high number of neutrons (eight instead of the usual six). This reaction may be written thus: $n_0^1 + N_7^{14} \rightarrow C_6^{14} + H_1^1$. The subscripts to these symbols refer to the nuclear charge or atomic number (i.e., the number of protons in the nucleus), while the superscripts refer to the number of nucleons (i.e., protons plus neutrons) in the nucleus. It will be seen that the above equation balances; that is both sides contain the same number of protons and the same number of neutrons.

Because the carbon-14 atoms formed have an unusually high number of neutrons, they are radioactive and decay with the emission of electrons (β-rays). However, they are relatively stable compared with some radioactive elements, having a half-life (see page 39) of between five and six thousand years. These radioactive isotopes of carbon, therefore, have plenty of time in which to combine with atmospheric oxygen (in the same way as ordinary carbon atoms), to form carbon dioxide (CO_2), and some of them will in due course be taken up by plants during photosynthesis (see page 105). Thus every tree will contain a certain number of radioactive carbon-14 atoms; not many, of course, but enough to make their presence known by the very sensitive methods of determining radioactivity (Geiger-Muller counters, etc.).

When a tree is cut down, it will cease to acquire further radio-carbon atoms and, as the radio-carbon atoms which it acquired during its lifetime decay, the number of these atoms present in dead wood will decrease with the passage of time. Therefore, by comparing the intensity of the radioactivity of a piece of modern wood with that of a piece of ancient wood of unknown age, the date of the latter can be calculated. This calculation must assume that the intensity of cosmic radiation over the last few thousand

7

years (a very short period of time compared to the life of the earth) has remained approximately constant. This assumption has been justified by checking the radioactivity of ancient wood specimens of known age from such sources as the tombs of the Pharaohs. In general, this ingenious method has been found to give reliable datings.

SUMMARY OF ELECTROMAGNETIC RADIATIONS

We have now examined briefly the properties and mode of emission of the various electromagnetic radiations. These results are summarized in Table 6.

THE VELOCITY OF LIGHT

During the course of our examination of electromagnetic radiations we have had occasion to mention that all such radiations, including light, travel through empty space at the same velocity of about 186,000 miles per second. As this speed is of the greatest importance in the universe it will now be necessary to say something about it. Firstly, it is an experimentally observed fact that the velocity of light is *absolute*, that is to say, it is not relative to the velocity through space of the measurer. To understand this statement let us consider the following examples.

Imagine two cars (Figure 46) travelling in the same direction

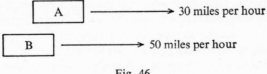

Fig. 46

along a road, one (A) at say 30 miles per hour, the other (B) at say 50 miles per hour. To an observer travelling in car A with an instrument for measuring the speed of remote bodies (about which we will say more later), car B would appear to be overtaking at a speed of 20 miles per hour. We say, in fact, that the speed of car B is 20 miles per hour relative to car A, although it is 50 miles per

Table 6

Name of radiation	Mode of emission	Characteristic property or use
Audio frequencies	Vibration of an electric or magnetic field by mechanical means	Transmission of sound by telephony
Radio frequencies	Oscillations of a current of electrons in a specially designed circuit	Transmission of modulated radio waves
Infra-red frequencies	Vibration or rotation of whole atoms or molecules	Transmission of radiant heat
Visible frequencies	Emission due to outer orbital electrons jumping from one energy level to a lower energy level	Visible light, light-sensitive reactions
Ultra-violet frequencies		Production of sun tan; ionization of upper atmosphere
X-rays	Emission due to inner orbital electrons jumping from one energy level to a lower energy level	Penetration of matter; medical diagnosis and radiotherapy; genetic mutation, etc.
γ-rays	Emission due to intra-nuclear disturbances	
Cosmic radiation	Arrival of high energy sub-atomic particles from outer space	Investigations of atomic nuclei; radioactive carbon dating

hour relative to the earth. It must not be forgotten, however, that the earth is rotating on its axis and also revolving in its orbit about the sun; furthermore, the solar system is in motion relative to the other stars within our galaxy, and the whole galaxy is in motion relative to other galaxies. Therefore the motions of the two cars *in space* are really very much more complex than they at first appear. In general, then, it will be seen that in order to specify the velocity of a body it is necessary to state to which other bodies this velocity is relative.

The velocity of light, however, is not subject to this reservation; it is not relative to any other motion in the universe, it is absolute. This can be further illustrated by a second example, but in this case it will be necessary to speed up one of the cars beyond the present limits of practical possibility.

Imagine, then, that car A is travelling at, say, 90 per cent of the velocity of light (about 167,000 miles per second), and that car B is stationary. If the driver of car B switches on his headlamp, just as car A passes him, the beam of light so produced will overtake car A because light travels at 186,000 miles per second (i.e., faster than car A). (Figure 47.) If the observer in car A uses

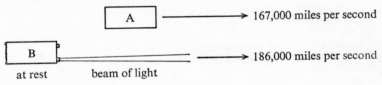

A ⟶ 167,000 miles per second

B ⟶ 186,000 miles per second

at rest   beam of light

Fig. 47

his speed-measuring instrument to measure the speed at which the beam of light is passing him he will find that it is *not* 186,000 − 167,000 = 19,000 miles per second, but the full velocity of light, namely 186,000 miles per second, i.e., the velocity of light is absolute and is not relative to the velocity of the observer.

This result appears to be quite contrary to our everyday experiences and seems at first to be altogether unintelligible, although if we were capable of moving about at these enormous speeds we should presumably be conditioned to reacting in a different way to such matters.

In fact, the explanation of this remarkable phenomenon is supplied by Einstein's Special Theory of Relativity, and is quite simple to understand in principle if one divests oneself of the erroneous conception of space and time with which we have become familiar in our everyday lives.

THE SPECIAL THEORY OF RELATIVITY

Having learnt what is meant by saying that the velocity of light is absolute, we shall now explain the far-reaching significance of this statement. In order to do so it must first be appreciated that a velocity is composed of a distance in space divided by an interval of time (for example, the number of miles travelled in one hour). So the speed-measuring instrument which we mentioned in our example of the cars must be capable of measuring both these quantities.

Furthermore, we must now rid ourselves of the preconceived idea that lengths or time-intervals are themselves absolute (that is, unchangeable). It must be accepted as an experimental fact that a rod which is one yard long when it is at rest, becomes shorter when its velocity is increased. This effect is negligible at our everyday velocities, but at velocities which approach that of light it becomes very important. This contraction of length with increasing velocity is called the Lorentz-Fitzgerald Contraction after the two discoverers, but its significance, as embodied in the *Special Theory of Relativity*, was first postulated by the late Professor Einstein. A similar phenomenon to the Lorentz-Fitzgerald Contraction is the slowing up of time with increasing velocity; thus a clock at rest may tick every quarter of a second, but the interval between each tick will become longer as the velocity of the clock through space is increased.

Bearing in mind these two facts, we can now understand the apparently unintelligible result we mentioned in the example of the two cars. In the second case the speed-measuring instrument in car A was travelling at 167,000 miles per second and therefore the lengths of its components would be appreciably shortened, and the clock mechanism it contained would tick more slowly than it did in the first example when it was travelling at 30 miles per hour. These changes combine to compensate exactly for the difference between the measured velocity of the light beam of 186,000 miles per second and the expected, non-relativistic velocity of 19,000 miles per second. (It must be made quite clear that the velocity of 19,000 miles per second would only be expected by someone who did not know the Theory of Relativity.)

Mass and Energy

As a result of the Special Theory of Relativity it can be shown mathematically that the contraction in length of a body as its velocity increases is accompanied by an increase in its mass. Again this effect is negligible at everyday velocities, but, for example, at 99 per cent of the velocity of light the mass of a body is about seven times greater than its mass at rest.

This increase of mass with velocity leads directly to the famous Einstein relationship between mass and energy: in fact, the mass of a body increases as a result of the additional energy which it acquires by virtue of its velocity.

The equivalence of mass and energy so derived is expressed by the simple equation: $E = mc^2$, where E = energy, m = mass, and c = velocity of light.

We see from this equation the importance of the velocity of light; it is, so to speak, the connecting link between mass and energy. Why this should be is unexplained; we can only say that this is the way the universe is constructed. The far-reaching effects of this mass-energy relationship are discussed in Chapter 11 on nuclear energy.

A further conclusion of the Special Theory of Relativity is that no body in the universe can travel at a speed equal to or greater than that of light, for in order to do so it would require an infinite amount of energy. This means that the velocity of light sets an upper limit to the rate of motion within the universe – it is a limiting velocity.

Space and Time

In the foregoing paragraphs we have shown that lengths and time-intervals are not absolute quantities, but are relative to the velocity of the measurers. This means that the conception of simultaneity must lose its significance. For instance, two events taking place at two widely separated points on the surface of the earth might appear to an observer at a third point on the earth to be simultaneous; they would not necessarily, however, appear to be simultaneous to an observer with a sufficiently strong telescope on Mars. This is because the earth and Mars are moving through space at different velocities, and as we have seen distances and time-intervals have different values for observers moving at different velocities.

To replace the conception of simultaneity, the Theory of

Relativity has been developed so that occurrences may be pinpointed in space and time in an accurate manner which takes into account the relative nature of lengths and time-intervals. In order to do this it has been necessary to abandon the usual way of thinking in terms of three dimensions of space and a separate dimension of time; instead we have to visualize a four-dimensional space-time continuum. On this subject a few words of explanation are required.

When in 1916 Einstein came to consider the wider significance of his Special Theory of Relativity he was forced, for reasons which would require a mathematical explanation, to think in terms of a system of geometry more widely applicable than that devised some 2,000 years ago by Euclid. In Euclidean geometry the basis of all the theorems is the straight line, to which is assigned the property that through a given point only one such line is possible which is parallel to another given straight line. Furthermore, in Euclidean geometry time has no place and has, therefore, to be considered independently from space.

For everyday purposes this system is adequate, but when interstellar distances and the velocities of atomic particles are considered Euclidean geometry loses its validity. Einstein was therefore forced to make use of a more widely applicable system of geometry, and for this purpose he adopted a system which had been invented by a mathematician called Riemann.

According to Riemann's geometry, space can no longer be considered independently from the phenomena which take place in it – it is therefore in some senses a fusion of geometry and physics. However, in the space so defined, the straight line loses its paramount significance, and space itself has to be regarded as being curved in such a way that the dimensions of the curvature depend on the distribution of masses within it.

Although it is somewhat difficult to visualize, it must be accepted that in order to define, spatially and temporally, any phenomenon in the universe, the definition, if it is to be valid under all circumstances, must locate the phenomenon in a four-dimensional space-time continuum within curved space.

Gravitation

The dependence of the shape of space upon the masses contained by it led Einstein to consider the forces of gravity, and to incorporate an understanding of these forces within what is known as his General Theory of Relativity.

So far we have said very little about gravitational forces, but we must now make a few remarks on this subject in order to explain Einstein's theory. In the seventeenth century Newton was able to explain the forces of gravity in terms of a simple law. He found that all bodies in the universe which exhibit the property of mass attract one another, and that the magnitude of the attractive force is proportional to the product of the masses and inversely proportional to the square of the distance between them. That is to say, the force (F) between two bodies of mass m_1 and m_2, separated by a distance (d) is given by the equation:

$$F = K \frac{m_1 \cdot m_2}{d^2}$$

where K is a universal constant.

It is, of course, the force of gravity which keeps the solar system together; for example, the earth remains in its orbit about the sun because the gravitational force between them exactly counterbalances the centrifugal force (the force developed by all bodies which move in a circular path). For similar reasons the moon and man-made earth satellites circle the earth in stable orbits.

The Newtonian explanation of gravity, however, gave no reason for its cause, it only described its magnitude. On the other hand, Einstein's General Theory of Relativity seeks to explain gravitation as a property of space. According to this interpretation, the presence of matter within space causes it to curve in such a manner that a field of gravitational forces is created. Once again this is a conception better expressed in mathematical equations (which are beyond the scope of this book) than in words.

This theory is clearly not the last word on the subject of gravitation, and in fact Einstein spent the last years of his life in an unsuccessful search for a unified field theory which would accommodate both the gravitational field and the electromagnetic field in one set of equations. Such a unified field theory is still the subject of present research, but no way has yet been found of fitting the conception of gravitation within the framework of the Quantum Theory which, as we have seen, is so necessary to an explanation of the electromagnetic field.

In addition to the two fields of force which we have mentioned there is a third field – the field of nuclear interaction which we shall have to discuss in the next chapter. It appears, at the present state of our knowledge, that these three fields are separate entities, but at the back of every physicist's mind is the hope that one day our understanding of nature will yield a system in which they will be integrated.

CHAPTER 11

NUCLEAR ENERGY

IN our analysis of the constitution of matter in Chapter 2 it was only necessary to give a very cursory outline of the structure of the atomic nucleus, because in that chapter we were discussing chemical reactions only. As we learnt then, in chemistry inter-actions between atoms are restricted to exchanges between orbital electrons: the nucleus itself remains intact. During the last twenty or thirty years, however, a whole new science of nuclear physics has developed as a result of which we are now able to bring about nuclear reactions which liberate enormous quantities of energy. We are familiar with this energy in the atomic bomb and the nuclear power station.

The energy which is liberated during nuclear reactions is a consequence of the conversion of matter into energy according to Einstein's equation, which he was able to show followed from his Special Theory of Relativity (see page 198). It will be remembered that in this equation, energy (E) is equated with the product of mass (m) and the square of the velocity of light (c): $E = mc^2$.

As the velocity of light is such a very large number, it follows from this equation that very little matter is required to create an enormous quantity of energy; in fact it is a simple calculation to show that the destruction of only one gram of matter would yield about one-and-a-half million horse power of energy for twenty-four hours. This mass-energy relationship remained a theoretical speculation until 1932 when the British physicists Cockroft and Walton carried out an experiment in which they used a stream of protons (hydrogen atom nuclei symbolized H_1^1) to bombard an isotope of the element lithium of atomic weight 7 (Li_3^7). The lithium nucleus was decomposed into a pair of helium nuclei (He_2^4, or α-particles): $H_1^1 + Li_3^7 \rightarrow 2He_2^4$. (We have already illu-strated equations of this type on page 193; it will be remembered that the subscripts refer to the nuclear charge while the superscripts refer to the number of protons plus neutrons in the nucleus.) This experiment was not only remarkable because of the artificial transmutation of the elements which had occurred, but because it gave experimental proof of Einstein's mass-energy equation.

The Mass Defect

In Cockroft and Walton's experiment it was found that the energy of the pairs of helium atoms was greater than that of the bombarding protons. This could only have occurred if energy had been created as a result of a loss of mass in the interacting nuclei. In fact the mass of the two helium nuclei was 8·0078 units (on the atomic-weight scale, see page 29), whereas the mass of the proton and lithium nucleus combined was 8·0261 units; there was therefore a loss of 0·0183 units.

This loss of mass, known as the *mass defect*, was found to be exactly equivalent, in accordance with Einstein's equation, to the energy gained in the process by the newly formed helium nuclei. In order to understand the source of this energy, and the way in which it is liberated, it will be necessary to examine the structure of the nucleus more closely.

The Neutrino

In Chapter 2 we said that the nuclei of all the atoms of the elements consisted of arrangements of only two types of particle, namely the proton and the neutron. We also said, when discussing radioactivity, that one of the emanations during radioactive decay was β-rays, which consist of streams of electrons. As the nucleus is too small to contain electrons, some further explanation is clearly needed.

This paradox was overcome by the prediction of a further sub-atomic particle which was given the name *neutrino*. This particle, as its name implies, has no charge and no mass when it is at rest, but it has the ability of carrying energy (and also 'spin' or angular momentum, which it is not necessary to discuss in this context).

With the aid of this particle, β-rays are explained as the emission of an electron (e^-) when a neutron (n) transforms into a proton (p), a neutrino (ν) being emitted at the same time: $n \rightarrow p + e^- + \nu$. We thus learn that protons and neutrons are not entirely separate particles, but according to the current view they may be regarded as different forms of the same entity, and the word *nucleon* is used to describe either of them.

The discovery of the neutrino also solved another problem concerned with the β-rays emitted by a radioactive source, as the following example illustrates.

There is a radioactive isotope of phosphorus, of atomic weight 32 (P_{15}^{32}), which decays to a stable isotope of sulphur (S_{16}^{32}) with the emanation of an electron (β-ray): $P_{15}^{32} \rightarrow S_{16}^{32} + e_{-1}$. Now the loss of mass during this decay should exactly equal the energy of the emitted electron on the Einstein mass-energy basis, but it was found that, in fact, the emitted electrons had a wide distribution of velocities giving them energies ranging from almost nothing up to the expected figure. There is therefore, on average, a deficiency of energy, which is made good by the postulation of the neutrino, for it is assumed that neutrinos emitted during β-decay have an energy compensating for the deficiency.

It must be added that having no charge, and no rest-mass, the neutrino is extremely difficult to detect, which accounts for the fact that it was not discovered until long after the nucleons.

NUCLEAR COHESIVE FORCES

So far, in our discussion of the nucleus, all the constituent particles which we have described have been either positively charged or electrically neutral; it would therefore be expected that the nucleus would fly apart as a result of the electrostatic repulsion which we have said always exists between two similarly charged particles. (It should be noted again, in this context, that the existence of electrons within the nucleus is not possible because the nucleus is simply not large enough to contain them.) In order to account for the cohesion of nucleons within the nucleus, therefore, a new class of particles was postulated by the Japanese physicist Yukawa in 1935, and their existence was subsequently confirmed as a result of cosmic-ray interactions (see page 191). The particles of this class are called *mesons*, and with their aid a different form of cohesion has been worked out based on *exchange forces*. Before elaborating on these new forces, however, it will be necessary to say something about mesons themselves.

Mesons

There are in fact several kinds of meson, some positively charged, some negatively charged, and some neutral. All, however, have a mass between that of the electron and the proton, and all are extremely unstable – the most durable meson exists for about one millionth of a second.

It is not necessary to go into the incomplete and somewhat complicated theory governing the decay and interchange of these particles; for the present purpose it is sufficient to say that the nucleus is to be thought of as being in a state of flux, in which cohesive forces are created by the 'exchange' of positive, negative, and neutral mesons between neutrons and protons which, as we have already seen, have the ability of changing into each other.

It has been said, by way of analogy, that, if the nucleons are regarded as the building bricks of the nucleus, the mesons are the cement which binds them together. It is admitted that there is still some difficulty in visualizing just what does happen within the nucleus, but it must be remembered that although we have spoken throughout this chapter of subatomic 'particles', we have been using the word more as an analogy than a precise description. Indeed, at a conference held in Rochester in 1960, some thirty subatomic particles were discussed although no coherent theory could be presented to account for their manifold interactions.

Exchange Forces

It is, however, usual to classify the interactions between subatomic particles into three groups: *strong interactions* between nucleons and mesons (*exchange forces*), *electromagnetic interactions* between protons and electrons, and finally *weak interactions* which result from the decay of neutrons as well as certain other processes which we need not detail.

The electromagnetic interactions, which account for the electrostatic repulsion between protons, fall off in effect as the particles come closer together; in fact at distances of less than 10^{-13} cm. the attractive exchange forces between protons and protons, and protons and neutrons, are some hundred times stronger than the electrostatic repulsive forces.

As nucleons within an atomic nucleus are packed together so closely that they may be regarded as almost touching each other, these strong exchange forces take over from the electrostatic forces and account for the cohesion of the nucleus. In this way central nucleons within the nucleus are pulled equally from all directions, while a nucleon at the surface is pulled only from the interior – a surface effect therefore develops so that, like a water droplet which experiences similar forces on the molecular scale, the nucleus adopts a spherical shape.

This surface effect is clearly much more pronounced in the smaller nuclei because they consist of only a few nucleons, a relatively high proportion of which are at the surface. With the larger nuclei, that is to say from about forty nucleons upwards, the electrostatic repulsion is a factor which has an appreciable effect, and therefore the nuclei are not so rigidly bound together. This accounts for the fact that the largest nuclei of all are not stable – in other words they are radioactive. As we shall see later, however, atomic bombs and nuclear power stations do not depend on natural radioactivity; for such purposes arrangements have to be made for breaking these heavy nuclei in two by bombarding them with neutrons, whereas during natural radioactive decay only fragments of the nucleus are thrown out in the form of α- and β-particles.

Binding Energy

We have said that the nucleus is held together very rigidly by exchange forces, and it is obvious that a considerable amount of energy must be linked with these forces. This is called the *binding energy* of the nucleus, and it is equal in magnitude to the mass defect which we have already mentioned. This will be apparent from the following remarks.

The constituents of a deuterium nucleus ('heavy hydrogen')

are a proton of mass 1·00758 units and a neutron of mass 1·00895 units, i.e., a combined mass of 2·01653 units. It is an experimental fact, however, that the mass of the deuterium nucleus is only 2·01419 units; that is to say, there is a mass defect when a proton and a neutron combine of 0·00234 units. This is equivalent to the energy holding the nucleus of deuterium together – its binding energy. It is also the energy required to break the nucleus into its constituents or conversely the energy evolved when the nucleus is formed.

For nuclei of up to about forty nucleons, in which we have seen that there is a pronounced surface effect, the addition of each nucleon increases the mass defect, and hence the building up of nuclei of less than forty nucleons leads to the evolution of energy. On the other hand, owing to the electrostatic effect, it is the breaking up of the heavier nuclei that leads to an increased mass defect and the evolution of energy. In other words, the *fission* of heavy nuclei or the *fusion* of light nuclei leads to the evolution of energy. We must now discuss separately each of these two methods of obtaining energy from the nucleus. We shall start with nuclear fission and follow with nuclear fusion.

NUCLEAR FISSION

We have given some explanation as to the reason for energy being liberated when a large nucleus disintegrates, and have said that in order to make use of this energy the nucleus has to be split in two by bombarding it with neutrons. It should be noted that neutrons make particularly effective nuclear missiles because they have no charge and are therefore not electrostatically repelled from their targets. Protons and α-particles have also been used for attacking the nucleus, but being positively charged they are repelled from it and are not, therefore, so effective as neutrons. (The nucleus as a whole is, of course, positively charged.)

In order to understand the working of the atomic bomb and a nuclear reactor as used in power stations for the production of electrical energy, we must now consider what happens when the heaviest of the natural elements, uranium, is bombarded with neutrons.

Isotopes of Uranium

Natural uranium consists of three isotopes of mass 234, 235, and 238 respectively. The isotope of mass 234 is present in only minute proportions and can for all practical purposes be disregarded. The 235 isotope is the most important, as we shall see later, although out of every 1,000 atoms of natural uranium only about 7 are of this isotope; nearly all the remaining 993 atoms are of the 238 variety.

If the 238 isotope of uranium (written U_{92}^{238} or just U^{238}) is bombarded by neutrons of all speeds, only the fastest-moving neutrons are able to break the nucleus into two approximately equal parts, i.e., to cause fission. On the other hand, this isotope has the ability of capturing a slow-moving neutron with the result that a fourth isotope of uranium of atomic weight 239 is formed. This isotope is, however, very unstable, having a half-life of only twenty-three minutes, and it decays by emitting an electron, thus gaining a positive charge. (It gains a positive charge because it has lost a negative charge.) The uranium-239 (U_{92}^{239}) is thereby transformed into a new element called neptunium of atomic number 93 and atomic weight 239 (Np_{93}^{239}). This new element is itself very unstable (half-life 2·3 days) and also emits an electron, becoming another new element, plutonium (Pl_{94}^{239}), which, although radioactive, is relatively stable with a half-life of 24,000 years. This sequence of events can be represented thus: $U_{92}^{238} + n_0^1 \rightarrow U_{92}^{239} \rightarrow e_{-1} + Np_{93}^{239} \rightarrow e_{-1} + Pl_{94}^{239}$. At this point we may note that, for the first time, we are discussing elements which have an atomic number in excess of 92. These elements, which are called for obvious reasons *Transuranic elements*, were not included in the list of elements given in Chapter 2 because they are not found in nature as their lives are far too short compared with that of the earth.

Now the transuranic element plutonium has a great deal in common with the 235 isotope of uranium as they are both fissioned fairly readily by neutrons of all speeds, but particularly by slow neutrons. Furthermore, each fission of a uranium-235 or plutonium nucleus into two approximately equal parts also creates between two and three fresh neutrons, which are in turn available to cause further fissions. Clearly, then, these two .

materials will sustain a *chain reaction* which will continue until all available nuclei have been fissioned.

The Atomic Bomb

The chain reaction which we have just described proceeds with explosive rapidity and the evolution of tremendous energy, as the survivors of the Hiroshima explosion can testify, for the atomic bomb dropped on Hiroshima consisted of some five to ten pounds of uranium-235, with an explosive effect equal to about 20,000 tons (20 kilotons) of TNT. Later models of the fission bomb employ plutonium to even greater effect, but these weapons are dwarfed by the hydrogen fusion bomb which we shall describe later.

Although this may be no place to air political arguments either for, or against, these appalling weapons, the writer of this book believes that no man of conscience should allow any opportunity to pass without condemning them absolutely and appealing for their total abolition. Scientists have unlocked for the world the secrets of nuclear reactions, and it is therefore their responsibility to see that they are used for the betterment of civilization and not its destruction.

With no apologies for these remarks, we may now return to the mechanism of the bomb.

It so happens that these two isotopes, uranium-235 and plutonium, are particularly suitable for military purposes, not only because they will sustain a chain reaction, but also because in quantities of less than a certain mass, called the *critical mass*, they are perfectly safe to store and handle.

The critical mass for uranium-235 is about three pounds; this is because a smaller lump, with its comparatively large surface area, will lose so many neutrons from its surface that there will not be enough within the body of the material to sustain a chain reaction. However, if the mass of material is increased, the surface area per unit of volume will be reduced, and as soon as the critical mass is reached there will be sufficient neutrons to keep the chain reaction alive. The atomic bomb is, therefore, constructed of two lumps of uranium-235, each with a mass less than the critical mass but greater than half the critical mass. When the bomb is fired these two lumps of uranium are brought together very rapidly, so that one lump in excess of the critical mass is formed. The chain reaction then proceeds and the bomb explodes.

It must be emphasized that even one stray neutron is sufficient to detonate a quantity of uranium-235 in excess of the critical mass, and there are always enough stray neutrons in the atmosphere for this purpose. as a result of cosmic ray reactions (see page 190). It is, therefore, essential to store uranium-235 and plutonium in quantities of less than the critical mass.

The Atomic Pile

The uncontrolled chain reaction which takes place in the atomic bomb is, of course, not suitable for the production of energy in an *atomic pile* (or *nuclear reactor* as it is perhaps more sensibly called) – far too much energy is released in far too short a time. The reaction therefore has to be tamed to produce energy at a much more leisurely pace.

Another important difference between the bomb and the reactor is that the former requires only a small quantity of fissionable material for its one devastating explosion, whereas the latter requires a steady supply of fissionable material which will produce energy day in and day out. Therefore the use of either plutonium or the rare uranium-235 would be prohibitively expensive: what is required is a method of using naturally occurring uranium, or naturally occurring uranium enriched with an extra quantity of plutonium or the 235 isotope.

Thermal Neutrons

The difficulty of using naturally occurring uranium is that, as we have seen, the common 238 isotope which forms the greater part of its bulk has the ability of capturing neutrons of certain speeds; many of the neutrons liberated by the fission of the small number of uranium-235 nuclei present will therefore be absorbed by the plentiful uranium-238 nuclei.

This obstacle to the use of natural uranium can, however, be overcome by greatly slowing down the free neutrons in the uranium material so that they have too little energy to be captured by the 238 nuclei, but sufficient energy to fission the 235 nuclei. Indeed, it is a happy coincidence that such very slow neutrons are the most efficient at bringing about the fission of 235 nuclei. Neutrons which have suitable energies to meet these requirements are called *thermal neutrons*, because their energies are so reduced that they are comparable to the thermal energies of the atoms amongst which they move. It must be stressed that thermal neutrons are very much less energetic than the slow neutrons captured by 238 nuclei.

The *thermalizing* (or slowing down) of neutrons is achieved by allowing them to collide repeatedly with light nuclei of other elements which do not either fission or capture them. Substances used for this purpose are called *moderators*, and it will now be necessary to say a few more words on this subject.

Moderators

In order to function usefully as a moderator for the thermalizing of neutrons, a substance must have the following properties:

1. It must not capture neutrons (for reasons which we have described).
2. It must consist of light atoms. Neutrons can be thought of in this sense as ping-pong balls; if a ping-pong ball collides with a relatively large object, such as a football, it will simply rebound without the loss of much energy, but if it collides with a ball more of its own size and weight, it will share a large portion of its energy with the other ball, the course and speed of which will be considerably altered. In the same way fast neutrons will only lose a substantial part of their energy by colliding with light nuclei.
3. A moderator must be available in the liquid or solid state, in order that it may be mixed with the uranium which is, of course, a solid. Helium, for example, would be a good moderator because it complies with the first two requirements, but as it is a gas which forms no compounds it cannot be used for this purpose.

The two substances which are most used as moderators at present, because they fulfil all these three requirements, are pure carbon, in the form of graphite, and heavy water (water formed from deuterium instead of hydrogen – formula D_2O). The earliest types of nuclear reactor consisted of slabs of natural uranium and slabs of graphite piled together (hence the name 'atomic pile') in a casing of graphite. More modern reactors consist of slabs of natural uranium enriched with uranium-235 immersed in a tank of heavy water. The heavy water can in this case be used as a cooling liquid for the extraction of the heat energy from the reactor as shown in Figure 48.

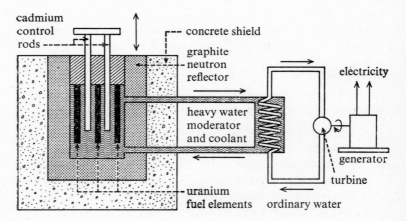

Fig. 48

Cooling Fluid

The heat energy liberated by a nuclear reaction is always collected by a cooling fluid which circulates through the reaction chamber. As this fluid becomes radioactive due to the neutron bombardment to which it is subjected, a closed circuit is usually employed so that the problem of disposing of large quantities of radioactive cooling fluid does not arise.

We have mentioned above that heavy water can be used as both moderator and cooling fluid. In such cases, of course, a closed circuit is used, the heat of the heavy water being transferred to ordinary water in a heat exchanger. The steam thus generated is used to drive a turbine, which in turn drives an electric generator. It will be seen, therefore, that in an atomic power station the nuclear reactor replaces only the boiler of a conventional power station. Other cooling fluids in current use are compressed carbon dioxide and a molten alloy of metallic sodium and potassium.

Control Rods

We have described in bare outline the principle of the nuclear reactor, in which the chain reaction of uranium-235 in natural uranium is propagated by neutrons which have been thermalized by the use of a moderator, but we have not mentioned the method of controlling the rate of reaction.

While it is true to say that the moderator controls the *speed* of the neutrons, and thus to a certain extent the progress of the reaction, the actual minute-to-minute control of the reaction is achieved by controlling the *number* of neutrons which are at large within the reaction vessel. For this purpose the metal cadmium is very suitable as it is an efficient capturer of neutrons. Therefore rods of cadmium (or cadmium-plated rods) are inserted into the reaction vessel, and the progress of the reaction is controlled by raising and lowering these rods in the reactor. If for any reason the reaction should get out of hand, the rods are fully lowered automatically so that the reaction is arrested.

Gamma-radiation and Shielding

Owing to the fact that most nuclear reactions are accompanied by the emanation of γ-rays, which are very dangerous to living organisms (see page 189), it is necessary to shield nuclear reactors inside a casing of concrete several feet thick. It is fortunate that concrete is a fairly efficient absorber of γ-rays and, at the same time, owing to the large number of hydrogen atoms which it contains, an effective capturer of any stray neutrons which may have escaped from the reactor.

Fission Products

When a uranium-235 nucleus is fissioned by a thermal neutron it is, as we have said, split into two smaller nuclei and two or three neutrons. The two nuclei formed are not necessarily of exactly equal size, nor in fact does every fission always produce the same end-products.

The commonest *fission products* formed have mass numbers (number of protons plus number of neutrons), around 90 and 140, but in all cases, of course, the total of the mass numbers of the two new nuclei and the two or three neutrons must equal 235. Similarly the atomic numbers of the two new nuclei must add up to 92. It is obvious then that, as the reaction progresses, the natural uranium will become increasingly contaminated with elements that have been created as a result of the fissions. Some of these elements may be innocuous, but some, such as the isotope of the rare gas xenon (Xe_{54}^{135}) are very effective neutron capturers and if allowed to remain in the fuel elements (as the sticks of uranium are called) would absorb sufficient neutrons to bring the chain reaction to a standstill. For this reason the fuel elements must be removed periodically so that the fission products can be extracted by chemical means. This operation has to be carried out by remote control, behind heavy shielding, as the fuel elements are extremely radioactive.

While fission products in general are detrimental to the operation of an atomic reactor, one in particular is beneficial – this is plutonium. We described earlier how plutonium is created as a result of the capture by a uranium-238 nucleus of a fairly slow neutron (but one that is still considerably more energetic than a thermal neutron). Although the moderator is present in the reactor to thermalize the free neutrons, some of them will collide with uranium-238 nuclei before they have had sufficient collisions with moderator atoms to be thermalized. For this reason a certain amount of plutonium will always be created in a reactor, and as it is fissioned by thermal neutrons in the same way as uranium-235 its presence in the fuel elements is advantageous to the progress of the reaction.

As plutonium is also required for the manufacture of bombs, it is usually extracted from the fuel elements when they are removed for purification. Indeed, some of the earlier reactors were constructed solely for the purpose of manufacturing plutonium for military uses, despite the fact that the quantity of plutonium formed is only of the order of one pound per ton of natural uranium.

Fast Breeder Reactors

Another type of nuclear reactor, now in operation at Dounreay in Scotland, is the so-called *fast breeder reactor* in which no moderator is used for thermalizing the neutrons.

This reactor consists of a small core of natural uranium enriched with plutonium, in which fast neutrons are allowed to produce a fairly fast chain reaction (but not of course as fast as the pure uranium-235 reaction of the bomb). Neutrons are allowed to escape from this central core into a surrounding blanket of natural uranium where some of them will be captured by uranium-238 nuclei with the consequent formation of plutonium. By suitable control of the conditions more plutonium can be produced in the natural uranium blanket than is used in enriching the core, and it is for this reason that the reactor is called a 'breeder'.

There is no doubt that fission reactors of one sort or another have a great future for the production of electrical energy throughout the world, and although several such reactors are currently in operation, they cannot yet be said to have passed their development stage.

Radioactive Isotopes

Nuclear reactors are not only useful for the production of energy and plutonium for military purposes; they also have a further use which is of great value.

If common elements are inserted into the neutron flux within a reactor, artificial *radioactive isotopes* of these common elements are frequently formed as a result of neutron capture. For example, common sodium (Na_{11}^{23}) forms a radioactive isotope of mass number 24: $Na_{11}^{23} + n_0^1 \rightarrow Na_{11}^{24}$.

Radioactive isotopes of this type have many industrial, biological, and medical uses because, while they are chemically indistinguishable from the common isotopes, their progress through a mechanical or biological system can be traced as a result of their radioactive emanations. Molecules containing artificial radioactive isotopes are said, for this reason, to be *labelled*. We have already mentioned the use of radioactive carbon-14 in the dating of wood of unknown age, due to the tree from which it came taking up labelled carbon dioxide from the atmosphere (see page 192). If such labelled carbon dioxide is mixed with ordinary carbon dioxide and fed to plants in the laboratory, the manner and speed of the incorporation of carbon into the structure of plants can be followed. This radioactive carbon will behave chemically in exactly the same way as ordinary carbon, because it differs from ordinary carbon only in the mass of its nucleus. Chemical behaviour, as we have seen, depends on orbital electrons and therefore upon the nuclear charge, not the nuclear mass.

A similar use to the tracing of radioactive carbon in plants, is the tracing of radioactive phosphorus in the bones of mammals. On the same principle radioactive iodine has been used for tracing the functioning of the thyroid gland and radioactive iron for examining the mechanism of blood formation. Many radio isotopes are also used for the treatment of medical conditions; for example, radioactive cobalt is of great benefit in the treatment of deep-seated cancer as it produces γ-rays of particularly suitable energy and intensity for this purpose. Industrially, radio isotopes have been used for a variety of purposes including the measurement of wear and the rate of flow of liquids.* These are only a few of the many uses of these extremely interesting by-products of nuclear energy.

FUSION REACTIONS

Having given a necessarily brief outline of the mechanism and uses of nuclear fission reactions, we may now pass to the second method of obtaining energy from the atomic nucleus, that is *nuclear fusion*. We have already said that the fusion of two light nuclei to form one heavier nucleus is attended by a substantial mass defect and the consequent evolution of an equivalent quantity of energy. It is from reactions of this type that the energy

*These uses are fully described in *Isotopes* by J. L. Putman (Penguin Books, Harmondsworth, 1960).

of the sun and the stars is derived – in particular, from the fusion of hydrogen nuclei to form helium.

This reaction does not take place directly, but in various stages involving the formation of deuterium (heavy hydrogen, D_1^2) and tritium (an unstable radioactive isotope of hydrogen the nucleus of which contains one proton and two neutrons, H_1^3). These fusion reactions may be summarized as follows:

$$H_1^1 + n_0^1 \rightarrow D_1^2$$
$$D_1^2 + D_1^2 \rightarrow H_1^3 + H_1^1$$
$$D_1^2 + H_1^3 \rightarrow He_2^4 + n_0^1$$

Each one of these reactions liberates vast quantities of energy, but none of them can be made to occur unless temperatures of several millions of degrees Centigrade are attained. This is because in order to bring these light particles close enough to each other to cause them to fuse, it is necessary for them to be accelerated to enormous speeds.

The Hydrogen Bomb

The only fusion reactions that have so far been brought about by man are those of the hydrogen bomb. This weapon consists of a normal uranium-235 or plutonium fission bomb surrounded by a layer of hydrogenous material. In this way the hydrogen nuclei are subjected to the extremely high temperatures required to initiate the fusion reactions mentioned above, and the neutrons which emerge from the fission core have sufficient energy to combine with the hydrogen nuclei. Reactions which occur at these temperatures are called *thermonuclear reactions*.

It should be noted that while fission bombs are limited in size by the critical mass effect which we have mentioned, hydrogen bombs can be made of virtually any size and destructive power. It will be remembered that the Hiroshima bomb was said to be equivalent to 20 kilotons (20,000 tons) of TNT – current models of the hydrogen bomb are rated at about 20 megatons (20 million tons) of TNT, while the Soviet Union has now tested a 50-megaton bomb.

THERMONUCLEAR REACTIONS

Physicists all over the world are currently trying to discover ways of harnessing the energy of thermonuclear reactions for peaceful uses. Such reactions have the great advantage over fission reactions in that they use as a fuel the plentiful element hydrogen, instead of the relatively scarce element uranium. The sea is full of water, every molecule of which contains two atoms of hydrogen!

However, the problem of containing within a vessel a reaction which takes place at several millions of degrees Centigrade has not yet been solved, although several attempts are being made at a solution. Of the various experimental devices that have been used to examine these thermonuclear reactions, one of the earliest was the British device known as Z E T A (Zero Energy Thermonuclear Assembly). This apparatus consists of a torus- (doughnut-) shaped vessel containing the gas mixture, to which an enormous voltage is applied in pulses of very brief duration. These pulses ionize the gas mixture, which in the ionized state is called a *plasma*, and raise its temperature to some million degrees Centigrade for a tiny fraction of a second.

In this sort of apparatus the problem of keeping the gas away from the walls of the vessel is partly solved for us by nature, for the current itself creates a very strong magnetic field which tends to confine the hot plasma to the centre of the tube. This contraction of the plasma, under the influence of a magnetic field, is called the *pinch effect*.

Unfortunately, however, the column of gas in the centre of the tube is not stable and tends to develop kinks, and therefore additional magnetic fields have to be provided from the outside in order to stabilize it.

These experiments have not yet met with complete success, and they have not so far provided a method of extracting the energy from the reaction. Z E T A was designed to create only sufficient energy to sustain the reaction, but the experiments have not fully realized the hopes of those who designed them.

The extraction of energy from thermonuclear reactions (once they have been made to take place under controlled conditions) presents a formidable and entirely unprecedented set of problems. It is hoped that, eventually, a way will be found for extracting electrical energy directly from the reaction without the cumbersome intermediary of steam-generating equipment, turbines, and generators. No work has yet been done on this aspect of the problem, but it is hoped that within the next few decades man will have been able to imitate the energy-producing mechanism of the stars, and so provide himself with an abundant and cheap supply of energy for his betterment and prosperity.

Undoubtedly thermonuclear reactions hold the key to the future development of our civilization. It is for the people of the world to decide whether this key shall be used to unlock the vast storehouse of free-for-all energy, or whether it shall be used to unleash the final devastating cataclysm of an H-bomb war.

PART FOUR

THE BOUNDARIES OF
KNOWLEDGE

CHAPTER 12

THE CREATION

IN the second and third parts of this book we have attempted to give a descriptive analysis of the nature and interrelation of the matter and energy which constitute the universe. This analysis has been based on evidence gained as a result of our sensory experiences, coupled with an ability to understand this evidence in terms of our deductive powers.

Every explanation which we have given has withstood the test of repeated experimental verification, but there are some phenomena which, either through lack of evidence or lack of understanding, we have been unable to fit into the general body of our knowledge. These are the topics which form the last part of this book, but before discussing them it is appropriate that we should repeat the qualification we made in Chapter 1; that is, scientific knowledge does not pretend to be absolute, it strives continually towards a deeper and more comprehensive understanding of the laws which govern the workings of the universe.

Firstly, then, we shall say something about those questions which, through lack of evidence, have puzzled man since his advent – these questions concern the creation of the universe, of the earth, and of life on earth. We shall then refer to some of the problems which, through lack of understanding, have eluded codification within our system of knowledge.

Before approaching the controversial subject of the creation, it would be as well to be somewhat more specific about our terms of reference and those of other systems which seek to explain these mysteries. Broadly speaking, attempts to answer fundamental questions dealing with the creation of the universe and the creation of life have, throughout recorded history, been of two kinds – the physical and the metaphysical.

The metaphysical approaches have postulated a supreme, and usually divine, creator whose ends and means have been either revealed to, or otherwise perceived by, selected individuals in an extra-sensory manner (e.g., mystical experiences, dreams, etc.). Those who have not had the benefit of such direct experiences have either accepted or rejected the 'evidence' of those who have as a matter of personal preference – acceptance, of course, being an act of faith rather than of reason. The chief disadvantage of this method, from a practical point of view, is that divinely revealed information must be accepted as absolutely true, that is, true for all time despite any evidence that may crop up to conflict with it. This dilemma has given rise to theology, which may be described as the art of fitting new evidence into old explanations.

Science, on the other hand, has no dogmatic beliefs of this kind, scientific knowledge, as we have seen, being self-correcting. Any fresh evidence that may appear either discredits or helps to confirm existing theories: if evidence builds up against a theory it is discarded and a better one sought in its place.

It is not the purpose of this book either to present or to criticize the metaphysical views concerning the creation, and having now mentioned the differences between the two systems, we may proceed to an outline of the current views of scientists which have been deduced from the meagre evidence available.

THE CREATION OF THE UNIVERSE

In Chapter 1 we briefly surveyed the distribution of matter throughout the universe, locating the earth in the solar system and the solar system in our galaxy of stars; we also said that there are countless millions of other galaxies distributed throughout the universe. Our problem now is to examine any available evidence which might give a clue as to the origin of the universe.

In Chapter 10 we mentioned one such clue – the shift towards the red of the light emitted by distant galaxies (see page 182). Now this evidence is extremely important as it seems to prove beyond doubt that all the distant galaxies are receding from us at enormous speeds. We must make it clear, however, that our galaxy, like most others, belongs to a local cluster of galaxies the components of which are not receding from each other – it is the distant clusters of galaxies which are receding from our local cluster. The rate at which these distant clusters are receding from ours – that is the rate at which the universe is expanding – has been measured spectroscopically with the somewhat startling result that the farther away a cluster of galaxies is, the greater is its observed speed of recession. In fact recently a very distant galaxy has been observed to be receding from us at nearly half the speed of light. Furthermore, from the evidence available, it now appears to be extremely likely that even more distant galaxies are receding from us at the speed of light itself, and therefore light from them can never reach us; such galaxies consequently cannot now form part of our real, that is observable, universe.

At this point it is necessary to say something about interstellar distances; so far we have referred to distances in terms of the terrestrial measure of a mile, but this unit is quite unsuited to the measurement of cosmic distances as it is far too small. Instead the *light year* is commonly used, which is simply the distance travelled by light in one year. As light travels at 186,000 miles per second (see page 150), a light year is equal to about 6 million, million miles. Even this unit is hardly adequate as a measure of cosmic distances because the most distant galaxies are several thousand million light years away from us. Astronomers also use another unit, the *parsec*. A parsec is the distance away one Astronomical Unit (mean distance of the earth from the sun) would be to subtend one second of arc. One parsec equals 3·26 light years.

Returning now to the origin of the universe, we must consider the two conflicting theories that have been developed from the clue that it is expanding. The first theory, known as the Super-dense Theory, suggests that if the universe is expanding at a known rate, it must be possible by a simple calculation to arrive at a moment of time in which all the matter and energy of which it consists was concentrated in one 'superdense' agglomeration.

A word of explanation is needed here: it must not be thought that the expansion of the universe implies that the earth is at its centre. Far from it – every cluster of galaxies is receding from every other cluster, without any one of them being at a centre. By way of analogy we may think of the atoms in an infinitely large crystal lattice as being the clusters of galaxies, so that if the crystal were to expand all the atoms would recede from each other.

8

According to the Superdense Theory, then, by working backwards from the observed rates of recession of the galaxies, it is found that they should all have been packed close together some seven or eight thousand million years ago. At about this time, it is postulated, there was a 'big bang' as a result of which the superdense agglomeration of matter and energy was scattered into multitudes of fragments, all travelling at different speeds, and in different directions, like fragments from an exploding bomb. The observed expansion of the universe is a continuation of this process which will presumably result ultimately in its dispersal, each component being for ever out of sight of its neighbours. Thus, as far as our cluster of galaxies is concerned, according to this theory, a time will come when we shall be alone in the observable universe.

This then is the Superdense Theory, and we must now mention a recently devised method of testing it. Although very distant galaxies are too far away for us to see with our optical telescopes, we are able to locate some of them with radio telescopes which collect the radio waves emitted by certain stars within them. Now if we are locating a star, say, 5,000 million light years away from us by the electromagnetic radiation which it emits, we must remember that we are locating it not as it is now but as it was when the radiation was emitted – that is, we are locating its position in space 5,000 million years ago. This being the case, it follows, according to the Superdense Theory, that the more distant galaxies, that is the ones we are seeing nearer to the time of the 'big bang', should be closer to each other in space than those which are nearer to us. Preliminary results of radio-telescope surveys of distant parts of the cosmos indicate that this is in fact the case. Although this is regarded as strong support of the Superdense Theory, it should be borne in mind that we do not yet know enough about the source of the radio waves emitted by some stars (but not others) for the evidence to be conclusive.

We now come to the second theory concerning the origin of the universe, whose adherents consider the Superdense Theory to be unsatisfactory in that it postulates a finite beginning, and possibly a finite end, for the universe. The second theory makes no such assumptions, as it proposes that matter is being continuously created throughout the universe. Thus matter which is lost by the recession of the distant galaxies is replaced by newly created matter, so that the observable universe is maintained in a steady state. This theory is accordingly known as the Steady State Theory.

Those who have propounded this theory have been able to show that by modifying the General Theory of Relativity (see page 200) the observed expansion of the universe can be accounted for as a result of the creation of matter, in the form of hydrogen, as a property of space itself. On this basis it has been calculated that the observed rate of recession of the galaxies would need to be compensated by the creation of one atom of hydrogen in a volume of space about the size of a fairly large house every thousand years. Such a rate of creation could not, of course, be observed, and therefore in order to decide which of the two theories is the closest approximation to the truth we shall have to wait until we are able accurately to assess the density of matter throughout the universe. For, as we have seen, according to the Superdense Theory it would be denser the farther away in distance (i.e., the farther back in time) we go, while according to the Steady State Theory it should remain approximately constant.

During the next few years we can expect to be able to answer this question one way or the other, which will give an enormous lead towards the solution of this most intriguing of all problems.

THE CREATION OF THE EARTH AND THE PLANETS

Having now given a resumé of the current theories concerning the origin of the universe, we may turn to the less controversial subject of the creation of the earth and the planets.

It used to be thought that the planets were lumps of matter which had been thrown out of the sun, but which had remained in its vicinity as a result of its gravitational attraction. However, with the invention of the spectroscope this theory ceased to be tenable as it was shown that the sun consists largely of hydrogen (over 90 per cent) and a small proportion of helium (about 8 per cent), while the earth, as we have seen, consists almost entirely of the heavier elements. In order, therefore, to understand the creation of the planets we must first examine the way in which the heavier elements (all the elements except hydrogen and helium) were created.

We have said that the greatest part of the matter of the universe consists of hydrogen, the simplest of the elements, the stars in the sky being very largely condensed masses of hydrogen. We also know that in the central regions of the stars hydrogen is compressed to such an extent that enormous temperatures are attained – temperatures of the order of several millions of degrees. In Chapter 11 we saw that at such temperatures thermonuclear reactions occur spontaneously converting hydrogen into helium with the evolution of prolific quantities of energy: this energy is transmitted through the body of the star to its surface whence it is radiated away in the form of light and other electromagnetic radiations.

Now although the temperature within the sun and other similar stars is sufficiently high to initiate the thermonuclear conversion of hydrogen into helium, it is not high enough for heavier elements to be formed, and consequently we have to look elsewhere for the source of these heavier elements. An important clue was provided by the discovery that not all the matter of the universe is concentrated in the stars: matter has also been found to exist in the form of highly rarefied clouds of hydrogen gas floating between the stars within a galaxy, and even in between galaxies. In fact the stars in their passages through space often pass through such clouds, replenishing their supply of hydrogen as they do so.

It has also been observed that, in addition to these clouds of pure hydrogen, there exist in space clouds in which the hydrogen is mixed with particles of dust. Indeed these dust-clouds are a great nuisance to astronomers as they obscure the stars which lie behind them. Nevertheless, they do provide a most significant clue to the origin of the heavier elements, for the presence of these solid particles floating through space indicates unequivocally the existence of non-gaseous heavy elements. It is now generally accepted that these heavier elements in the dust-clouds originated in certain exceptional stars called *supernovae*, which it will be necessary briefly to describe.

Through the ages of recorded astronomy it has been observed

that from time to time certain stars have suddenly and for no apparent reason flared up, increasing their brightness to such an extent that they become up to 100,000 times as bright as our sun. These stars are called *novae*, but they are comparatively unspectacular compared to the considerably rarer stellar explosions suffered by the so-called *supernovae*, which can increase their brightness so that they emit some 1,000 million times as much energy as the sun.

These supernovae have been observed in distant galaxies, but they are so rare that none has been observed in our own Milky Way since the invention of the telescope. There have, however, been two probable supernovae observed by the naked eye, one in 1604 and one in 1054. Of course, we cannot say for certain what causes a supernova, but it is confidently believed, as a result of the available evidence, that this phenomenon occurs when a star runs out of hydrogen – this causes it to shrink and therefore to increase its internal pressure and temperature. As a consequence of this increased temperature the heavier elements are formed by the thermonuclear transformation of hydrogen and helium but, as we saw in Chapter 11, the formation of elements with atomic numbers in excess of about 40 involves the absorption of energy and therefore a fall in temperature. The interior of the star is thus rendered insufficiently hot to maintain the internal pressure required for its stability; consequently it collapses, and as it does so its rate of rotation increases to such an extent that material is flung from its surface. In this way the hot interior is exposed, which causes the observed increase in brightness. Finally, when the supernova has discharged most of its matter (in the form of the heavier elements) into space, it settles down as a small bright star of high density which is known as a *white dwarf*.

This process could account for the presence in interstellar space of gas-clouds containing dust particles of the heavier elements. To account for the formation of the planets of our solar system, the most reasonable assumption to make is that the sun at one time had a companion star revolving around it which suffered the fate of becoming a supernova. Such double-star systems are extremely common, in fact it is estimated that half the stars in the universe are associated with one or more companion stars. It has been calculated that if such a supernova exploded at a distance from the sun approximately equal to the present distance of the planet Jupiter, only a very small fraction of the matter thrown out by the explosion would be required to be trapped by the sun's gravitational field in order to provide sufficient material for the creation of all the planets.

Initially this material would have been at a very high temperature, and would have spread out into a great flat disk of vaporized heavy elements in the plane of the present orbits of the planets. As the material in the disk cooled, however, the atoms would condense together forming small dust particles which, over the ages, as a result of constant collisions, would be expected to aggregate into larger and larger planetary bodies. It is considered unlikely that the present nine planets and the asteroids are the original agglomerations; they may rather be the present manifestation of the break-up of larger and fewer planetary bodies. This breaking up of larger planetary bodies would account for the position of the three inner small planets (see page 15) of which the earth is one. As for the white dwarf which represented the residue of the exploding supernova, it must be assumed that as a result of the recoil of its explosion it broke free from the sun's gravitational field and flew off into space.

This explanation of the creation of the planets may seem somewhat hypothetical, which indeed it is, but like any other scientific theory, it fits all the observed facts as they now appear, and it will therefore survive unless any new evidence arises which will require its modification or replacement.

THE CREATION OF LIFE

We now come to consider the question of the creation of life on earth, a subject which we have already mentioned in Chapter 6 when we encountered the difficulty of defining matter which is living. It will be remembered that we accepted then, as a basis for discussion, the cell as the unit of life, and described the virus as a likely step in the direction of the cell. However, it must not be overlooked that the virus, as we know it today, cannot itself be regarded as the forerunner of the cell, because it requires a host-cell in which to live. Nevertheless, a single sub-cellular type of large molecule of the virus type seems a most probable stage in the development of the cell.

The problem, then, is to try to visualize the sort of processes which, taking place on the newly formed earth consisting presumably of only simple inorganic molecules, led to the formation of the intensely complex proteins and polynucleotides which are the raw materials of life as we know it today.

As a first step, there is a certain amount of evidence that such simple molecules as water, methane, and ammonia can be built up into amino acids (see page 101) by the action of the sun's ultra-violet radiation; furthermore, it is considered likely that these simple molecules were present in substantial quantities in the atmosphere of the young earth.

In Chapter 6 we said that in living organisms the combination of amino acids to form proteins requires the catalytic effect of enzymes (which are themselves proteins), but there is no reason to suppose that this is the *only* way – the fact that it is undoubtedly the best and quickest way does not preclude a slower and more inefficient means from having initiated the process. It has been suggested that such catalytic surfaces as air/water interfaces or wet clay may well have been suitable for the purpose.

Once molecules as complex as proteins had been formed on the earth, the stage would be set for the formation of nucleo-proteins capable of self-duplication. Such molecules would then be able to multiply until their environment ceased to contain the appropriate ready-made components – self-duplication would then cease until by some accident (e.g., mutation) some molecules acquired the ability of catalysing the production of the essential missing component from its constituents. Molecules possessing this ability would thrive and evolution by natural selection would have begun.

Eventually some of these self-duplicating virus-like molecules may be imagined as forming symbiotic relationships with each other, so that orderly systems of separate molecules would group together, dividing between them the labour of manufacturing the materials required for their duplication. Such systems of molecules may then be imagined as existing in a medium consisting of the materials resulting from their metabolic processes. It is in some such way as this that the evolution of cells is envisaged – the self-duplicating molecules developing into the nucleus, and their metabolic environment becoming the cytoplasm. Such theories are necessarily of a speculative nature and many variants and amplifications of the above outline have been suggested.

However, there is no evidence to support the view that animation only occurred at one time and place, making us all descended from one molecule that acquired the ability to live. If we allow that life may have been created not once but many times, and in many places, we are led to the question of whether or not new life is still being created from the inanimate. This is a matter over which there is a good deal of controversy, although there is no evidence either for or against the proposition. This is not surprising as any newly formed primitive organism, at the present stage of evolution, would almost certainly be consumed by, or at least unable to compete with, more highly developed and well-established organisms. It must not be forgotten that when life first appeared on earth it was a very different planet from that with which we are now familiar: the two principal destructive forces of nature, oxidation and bacterial decay, were totally absent. The earth's atmosphere largely became oxidizing as a result of the oxygen liberated by plants during photosynthesis, and bacterial decay had to await the arrival of bacteria. Thus the first life-forms would have been born into a considerably less destructive and competitive environment than any newly created life could expect to find today.

Before leaving this subject, it should be mentioned that a theory has recently been proposed which postulates that life may not have originated on the condensed earth, but may have been created at an earlier stage in the history of the planets. Indeed, it is quite possible that suitable conditions for the building up of large organic molecules could have occurred when the heavy elements were still in the form of dust particles, or small agglomerations, circling the sun. The recent discovery of traces of organic compounds on a meteorite has given some support to this theory, but as the meteorite fell to earth during the last century, the possibility of contamination on earth cannot be ruled out.

This theory leads inevitably to the question of whether life exists elsewhere in the universe, either within the solar system or outside it. Here the evidence is very sparse indeed: it can be said that climatic conditions on our neighbouring planets, Venus and Mars, are such that life is just conceivable; in fact the spectroscope indicates the presence on Mars of organic compounds – not necessarily, of course, animate. However, speculation on this subject is somewhat pointless, especially as it should not be too long before space vehicles capable of sending back the relevant information have been landed on Mars.

As regards life outside the solar system, we have no evidence at all – no evidence even of the existence of planetary systems. All we can say is that, taking into account the gigantic number of stars in the universe, it would be most surprising if our sun were the only one to be favoured with a system of planets. Furthermore, if there are as many planetary systems as one would expect, it is extremely probable that a great many of them have individual planets, with similar temperatures and climatic conditions to ours, on which life could have developed. It must be remembered that the whole universe, so far as we know, is constructed from the ninety-two elements with which we are familiar on earth, and their chemistry will be the same wherever they are.

In concluding this chapter it is perhaps appropriate to say once more that science is continually moving forward. Even twenty years ago it would have been almost inconceivable to imagine that space vehicles could tell us whether or not life exists on Mars within our lifetime. In the same way, new evidence may come in the future from totally unexpected quarters to help us solve what now appear to be unanswerable questions concerning the creation.

CHAPTER 13

THE NATURE OF MATTER

HAVING discussed some of the problems to which we are not
able to give a definitive answer through lack of evidence, we now
pass on to look at some of those subjects at the boundary of our
knowledge which we are unable to answer through lack of understanding.

The first of these may be simply put: what is matter? Although
we have devoted over half this book to describing the properties
of matter, our only attempt at a definition has been to say that
matter is a specialized form of energy which possesses the
attributes of mass and extension in space. However, the view has
recently been expressed that perhaps this is not enough – that
matter is more than simply another name for energy.*

That the mass of an atom at rest is a form of energy has been
proved by nuclear transformations and the liberation of energy
equal to the mass defect, but the view that matter may be something more than energy is to some extent supported by the
observation that elementary particles can be divided into two
separate classes: *fermions* and *bosons*. Fermions are further subdivided into two groups, nucleons and hyperons belonging to one
group called *baryons*, electrons, positrons, and neutrinos belonging to the other group called *leptons*. These two groups, baryons
and leptons, are distinguished from each other in that members
from one group cannot transform into members of the other
group. Furthermore, all fermions are characterized by the fact
that their numbers are conserved throughout all nuclear interactions. The number of bosons, on the other hand, which include
photons and some mesons, is not conserved.

This diversity in the fundamental properties of elementary
particles seems to imply that matter, which is of course made up
of both fermions and bosons, cannot be simply regarded as
consisting of the energy of the particles concerned. However, at

* Sir G. P. Thomson, The British Association, September 1960.

this point we are at the limit of our understanding; indeed, as we have already said, a coherent system has not yet been formulated which satisfactorily explains the abundant evidence concerned with the sub-nuclear particles and their interactions.

A further difficulty concerning our understanding of the structure of matter arises from doubts as to the 'elementarity' of some of these particles. Recent scattering experiments with very high-energy electrons have indicated that protons themselves seem to have a structure, consisting of a central core surrounded by a cloud of pi-mesons. Thus, as Professor A. Salam has said, 'All particles are elementary, but some are more elementary than others.'*

Perhaps some of the difficulty which we experience in failing to understand the fundamental properties of the constituents of matter is attributable to the inadequacy of language. Inevitably, our words and the meaning we ascribe to them are a reflection of our everyday experiences; we must therefore expect them to be ill-adapted to the description of entities which, both by virtue of their size and nature, do not fall within the scope of these experiences. Thus, to describe, say, an electron as either a 'wave' or a 'particle', is as we have already said no more than an analogy. It is clearly neither the one nor the other; it is something for which we have no word. For this reason the question 'What is an electron?' becomes somewhat rhetorical. We shall return to this question of meaning and the questions it is sensible to ask shortly; before doing so we must say something about 'anti-particles' and their logical consequence – anti-matter.

ANTI-MATTER

We have already described the first anti-particle to be discovered, the positron (see page 191); it will be remembered that this entity has an identical mass to an electron, but an opposite charge. In 1955 the Bevatron 'atom smasher' (at Berkeley, U.S.A.) produced a new particle whose existence had been predicted some years earlier. This particle has the same mass as a proton, but being negatively charged is called an *anti-proton*. More recently still

Penguin Science Survey, 1961, vol. 1.

anti-neutrons and anti-neutrinos have been observed, so that there is no theoretical reason why anti-matter should not be built up from these anti-particles.

This remains, however, something of an academic proposition on our earth – even if we were able to join an anti-proton with a positron to make an atom of anti-hydrogen, it would be difficult to know what to do with it, because a particle and its anti-particle annihilate each other on collision with the production of energy. As everything on earth is constructed of matter, anti-matter would stand considerably less chance of survival than the proverbial snowball in hell. Nevertheless, as anti-matter probably has an identical structure to that of matter, there is no logical reason for supposing that parts of the universe (distant galaxies, for instance) could not be made of it. This is, however, a matter for speculation.

Finally on this subject we may note that, according to the Special Theory of Relativity, a negative electron has a positive kinetic energy, which causes it to move through the four-dimensional space-time continuum from past to future. On the other hand a positive electron has a negative kinetic energy which would appear to mean that it travels backwards through time from future to past. Whether such a state of affairs has any real meaning, or whether it is no more than a mathematical mis-understanding, we cannot yet say. It is, however, an interesting point, which leads us back to the question of 'meaning' and the sort of questions which it is sensible to ask.

CAUSALITY AND PROBABILITY

We have said that there are some questions which the failure of language make it difficult for us to answer; as we shall now see, there are also some questions which it is meaningless to ask. For example, in Chapter 11 we mentioned the Heisenberg Uncertainty Principle, according to which we are precluded from knowing both the position and velocity of the ultimate particles of nature (i.e., particles small enough to be governed by quantum considerations). Therefore, if we know, say, the velocity of an electron, it is meaningless to ask, 'Where precisely will it be at a given instant of time?' Admittedly the question sounds reasonable enough at the common-sense level, but as it demands a piece of information which our relationship with the universe precludes us from possessing it is without meaning.

It must be accepted, then, that some apparently sensible questions lose their meaning at the profoundest level, and we must admit that we cannot expect to know everything about the universe with unlimited precision. This brings us to the question of *causality*. According to the Laws of Classical Physics (physics before the invention of the Quantum Theory), every 'effect' in nature was held to be the result of a definite 'cause': every occurrence was regarded as being predictable if the conditions preceding it could be precisely described. This is the Law of Causality.

Let us look at an example: we say that roulette is a game of 'chance', by which we mean that we cannot predict into which of thirty-seven holes the revolving ball will fall. But we must be clear that in this case we are using the word 'chance' to conceal our inability to calculate the various factors which control the course of the ball. If we could measure with precision the initial momentum of the ball and the wheel, and if we had an accurate knowledge of the friction forces between them, we would be able to predict with certainty where the ball would come to rest. Clearly, however, to do so is not a practicable proposition and to all intents and purposes the final position of the ball depends on chance. But because the outcome could in theory be predicted the Law of Causality is not broken.

It is only when we try to apply these strict causal rules to the behaviour of sub-atomic particles that we find that they break down. The reason for this is easy to see: we never know precisely where these particles are. All we can do, as we have already said, is to express their positions as a *probability* that they will be found in a particular area of particular wave-trains. Clearly, once we have admitted that we cannot be sure where a particle is, we must automatically relinquish our claim to knowing what will become of it in the future. To be precise, we must even admit that consecutive observations of what we may imagine to be the same electron may in fact be observations of two separate electrons. For if a particular particle cannot be precisely located it is not reasonable to be able to claim to have established its identity.

Thus the whole basis of causal relationships and the certainties they imply is completely undermined and must be replaced by the conception of probabilities which is inherent in the Quantum and Wave Theories. For example, as we mentioned in Chapter 2, natural radioactive decay is a non-causal, or indeterminate, occurrence – there is no way of knowing when a radioactive atom will break down because it is purely a matter of chance. We may express the chance as a probability, and over a large enough number of atoms this probability becomes a near certainty, but it is still fundamentally a probability.

In conclusion it must be added that some physicists, including the late Professor Einstein, have not accepted as final these indeterminate interpretations of nature. Indeed, it is by no means impossible that a unified theory will one day be discovered to include both relativity and quantum phenomena, which will revert to the causality of classical physics by showing that the probabilities of quantum mechanics simply conceal our ignorance of the truly causal nature of reality. This is a horizon for scientists of the future.

EPILOGUE

At the beginning of this book it was said that our approach to the subject of science was to be exclusively descriptive; that is, we have not attempted to illustrate the crucial part played by experiment, measurement, and mathematics – the three essential steps in a quantitative assessment of natural phenomena.

The descriptive approach has been adhered to throughout, because this book is not intended for the professional scientist whose job it is to carry out these experiments and measurements, but rather for the layman who wishes to understand the ideas deduced from them. However, it should be appreciated that the exclusion of both the quantitative and the historical approach has made it impossible to illustrate the extent to which the development of scientific knowledge and understanding has depended upon man's ability to make measurements of ever-increasing precision. In fact, nearly all the great theories of science (e.g., the Relativity and Quantum Theories) have been developed as a result of small discrepancies between experimentally measured values and the mathematical predictions of existing theories. It is therefore appropriate that this aspect should be mentioned lest its importance should be overlooked.

Another defect of the purely qualitative approach is that sometimes the language of words is unable to communicate concepts that have their origin in the language of mathematics – in such cases, therefore (e.g., wave mechanics and General Relativity), we have been rendered almost totally inarticulate.

Nevertheless, it is hoped that the reader will have found that the benefits of the descriptive approach have outweighed its defects.

INDEX

Acetylenes, 73, 74
Acids, 49
Actinons, 57, 60
Air, 25, 41, 135
Alcohols, 75
Aldehydes, 77
Aliphatic compounds, 69–79
Alkalis, 50
Amines, 79
Amino acids, 101, 102
Amplifiers, 157–8
Anabolism, 100
Anti-matter, 235–6
Anti-neutrino, 236
Anti-neutron, 236
Anti-proton, 235
Aromatics, 80
Asteroids, 16
Atom, 21, 22–39; the Bohr, 173–174
Atomic nucleus, 26, 27–8, 36–7
Atomic number, 29
Atomic pile, 210
Atomic structure, 26–31
Atomic weight, 29
Avogadro's Hypothesis, 41

Bacteria, 92
Baryons, 234
Bases, 50
Binding energy, 206–7
Biochemical reactions, 99–101, 103–20
Biochemistry, 88
Biology, 88
Boiling-point, 43, 133
Bomb, atom, 209–10; hydrogen, 217

Bosons, 234
Broadcasting, 158–66
Brownian movement, 42

Calorie, 133
Carbohydrates, 105, 106–9; metabolism of, 109–13
Carbon cycle, 62
Carboxylic acids, 76, 82
Catalysts, 68, 100, 231
Causality, 236–8
Cell, living, 89–92, 231; electric, 139–40
Chlorophyll, 99, 105
Chromatids, 90, 121
Chromosomes, 90, 120, 121, 122
Citric-acid cycle, 112, 115, 117
Coal tar, 80
Combination, chemical, 32–6; covalent, 34; electrovalent, 33
Combustion, 135
Compounds, 22
Conduction, ionic, 34
Cosmic radiation, 94, 190–3
Creation of the earth, 227–30
Creation of life, 230–3
Creation of the universe, 224–7
Critical mass, 209, 217
Crystals, 43–6
Cyclic compounds, 80–3
Cytoplasm, 89, 90, 121, 232

Deoxyribonucleic acid (DNA), 120, 123
Deuterium, 28, 206, 212, 217
Drosophila, 92

Earth, the, 14, 230; age of, 88; composition of, 22
Efficiency, 137, 138
Electrodes, 139
Electrolysis, 140
Electrolytes, 139
Electromagnetic radiation, 151, 153ff.; summary of, 195
Electromotive force, 140
Electron, 26, 27, 128, 139–40, 186, 188
Electron microscope, 122, 178
Electron shells, 30–3, 173–4
Elements, 22, 23, 52–68; Table of, 23, 54; transition, 56; transuranic, 57, 208
Energy, in biological systems, 103, 104; chemical, 131–3; conservation of, 130, 134; electrical, 139ff; forms of, 128, 129; heat, 132, 133–5; kinetic, 128, 131, 136; mechanical, 135–8; nuclear, 131, 202ff.; potential, 128, 131; radiant, 132, 153ff.
Entropy, 136, 137
Enzymes, 100–1, 108, 120
Equations, chemical, 25, 132
Esters, 75, 77
Ethers, 76
Evaporation, 42
Evolution, 92–9
Exchange forces, 205–6

Fats, 77, 105, 113
Fermions, 234
Field, electric, 142; electromagnetic, 146–9; gravitational, 200-201; magnetic 142–6
Fission, nuclear, 207ff.
Fission products, 213–15
Freezing-point, 43

Fuels, fossil, 61, 62, 135
Fusion, nuclear, 216ff.

Galaxies, 17, 224–7
Gamete, 95
Gases, 40, 41, 131; inert, 31, 32; Kinetic Theory of, 40
Genes, 90, 93, 94, 120, 122
Geometry, 199
Glycolysis, 111
Gravitation, 200–1

Half-life, 39, 193
Heat energy, 132, 133–5
Heat engine, 135
Heat pump, 134
Heisenberg Uncertainty Principle, 175, 178, 236
Hormones, 103, 118
Hyperons, 234

Induction, electromagnetic, 146
Inheritance, genetic, 90, 120–2
Ionosphere, 159, 185
Ions, 34, 45, 49, 159
Isomerism, 72
Isotopes, 28

Katabolism, 100
Ketones, 78

Lanthanons, 57, 60
Leptons, 234
Life, definition of, 88; origin of, 88, 92, 230–3
Light, colour of, 172; emission of, 172–3; interference of, 175–176; refraction of, 170–1; velocity of, 149, 194ff.
Light year, 225
Lipids, 113, 114; metabolism of, 115

Liquids, 41–3
Lorentz-Fitzgerald Contraction, 197

Magnetism, 142–6
Mass, conservation of, 130, 133, 134
Mass defect, 203, 206, 207
Mass–energy relationship, 13, 128, 132, 134, 197–8, 202–3
Matter, nature of, 21ff.; physical states of, 40ff.
Mesons, 192, 204–5, 235
Metabolism, 99–100, 105–18; control of, 118
Metazoa, 98
Milky Way, 17
Mitochondria, 90, 118
Mitosis, 90
Mixtures, 25
Moderators, 211–12
Modulation, 160
Molecules, 24; diatomic, 25, 131
Moon, 16
Mutation, genetic, 94, 120

Neutrino, 203–4
Neutrons, 28, 30, 193, 207ff.; thermal, 210–11
Nitrogen cycle, 64, 65
Novae, 229
Nuclear cohesion, 204ff.
Nuclear weapons, 190, 209–10, 217
Nucleon, 193, 204, 206, 234
Nucleotides, 104, 121, 123
Nucleus of atom, 26, 27–8, 36–7, 203ff.
Nucleus of cell, 89–92, 120–2, 232

Ohm's Law, 141
Olefins, 73

Oxidation, 51, 135
Oxides, 51, 52, 64

Paraffins, 70–2
Parsec, 225
Peptides, 102
Periodic table, 31, 52, 54–5; groups of, 53, 58–68
Phosphates, 64, 104
Photo-electric effect, 183–4
Photons, 174, 187, 188, 192
Photosynthesis, 61, 96, 105–6, 232
Pinch effect, 218
Planck's Constant, 168–9, 177
Planets, 14, 15, 230; distances from sun, 15
Plasma, 218
Polymerization, 73, 86
Polymers, 73, 83–7
Polynucleotides, 121, 122
Polypeptides, 102
Polysaccharides, 107, 108
Positrons, 191–2, 235
Probability, 178, 236
Proteins, 101–3, 231; metabolism of, 115, 117
Protons, 27, 30, 203–4, 235
Protoplasm, 89
Protozoa, 98

Quantum, energy of, 127, 128, 168–9, 186
Quantum Theory, 127, 168, 174, 201, 238

Radar, 166
Radiation, alpha, 36; beta, 37, 203–4; cosmic, 94, 190–3; gamma, 37, 94, 184, 185, 192, 213; infra-red, 166–9; ionizing, 94, 188–90; ultra-violet, 184–5

Radicals, inorganic, 48, 49; organic, 74
Radio receivers, 164–6
Radio transmitters, 161–3
Radio waves, 153–4
Radioactive isotopes, 193, 204, 215–16
Radioactive series, 37
Radioactivity, 36–9, 193, 238
Radio-carbon dating, 192–4
Reactions, chemical, 25, 132; endothermic, 132; exothermic, 132, 135
Reactors, fast breeder, 215; nuclear, 212–15
Reduction, 51
Refraction, 170–1
Relativity, general, 200–1; special, 196–9, 236
Reproduction, genetic, 90–2, 120–122
Resins, synthetic, 83–7; thermoplastic, 85, 86; thermosetting, 84, 85
Resonant circuits, 161–2
Ribonucleic Acid (RNA), 122, 123
Ribosomes, 121, 122

Salts, 50, 51
Shift towards the red, 182, 224
Silicones, 63
Solar system, 14, 191, 200, 227–30
Solids, 43–6
Sound, characteristics of, 154–5; velocity of, 155
Space-time continuum, 198–9
Spectra, absorption, 181–2; emission, 179–80
Spectroscope, 182, 185

Spectrum of electromagnetic radiation, 151; visible, 170
Steady State Theory, 226–7
Steroids, 114
Sulphanilamides, 81, 101
Sun, 16, 185, 227–30
Superdense Theory, 225–6
Supernovae, 229
Symbiosis, 109, 231

Temperature, 46, 133; absolute zero of, 47, 137
Theology, 224
Thermodynamics, 134; Laws of, 134–7
Thermonuclear reactions, 217–19, 228
Transistors, 157, 158, 165

Unified Field Theory, 200–1, 238
Uranium series, 38

Valency, 35–6
Valve, electronic, 157–8
Vapour pressure, 43
Viruses, 88, 122, 123, 230

Water, 24, 25, 43, 46, 51, 66
Wave-lengths, 149; Table of, 151, 153
Wave mechanics, 178, 238
Waves, electromagnetic, 148–50; longitudinal, 155; sound, 154–6; transverse, 155

X-rays, 94, 120, 185ff.; emission of, 186; production of, 187

Zeta, 218
Zygote, 95